Love...

Quilting

Love...

Quilting

18 Simple Step-by-Step Projects to Sew

IMM lifestylebooks™
Read. Learn. Do What You Love.

Published 2016—IMM Lifestyle Books
www.IMMLifestyleBooks.com

IMM Lifestyle Books are distributed in the UK by Grantham Book Service.

In North America IMM Lifestyle Books are distributed by
Fox Chapel Publishing
1970 Broad Street
East Petersburg, PA 17520
www.FoxChapelPublishing.com

10 9 8 7 6 5 4 3 2 1

ISBN 978 1 5048 0026 6

Printed in Singapore

Contents

Introduction

Although there is evidence that pieced or patchwork quilts were used as early as the 1600s, the craft is probably most frequently associated with the pioneering Settlers making a new life in America. Of necessity they used every scrap of fabric available to make quilts to keep their families warm in the harsh winters. It is probable that the pieced "blocks" so associated with American patchwork were first created to enable them to stitch while making the long journeys to find a new home. During the bicentennial celebrations of the American Independence there was a great resurgence of the craft, which in turn spawned the enormous worldwide quilting industry of today.

This industry and the quilters who feed it have created the many and varied tools which make the craft so much easier and faster today. These tools not only enable patchwork to be assembled with the speed that the world finds so essential now, but they also produce a greater accuracy in the cutting and piecing of individual components that make up a patchwork quilt.

The quilts in this book all make use of these tools and techniques. Each one explores a variety of traditional and modern methods including appliqué and other surface embellishment, as well as machine quilting. The projects range from bed quilts and throws to wall hangings and table runners. Whether you prefer to use fat quarters or jelly roll strips, or simply have a stash of leftovers to use up, the quilts here have been designed to work with these small units of fabric. The projects are designed for quilters of all skill levels and all techniques are clearly explained.

the Basics

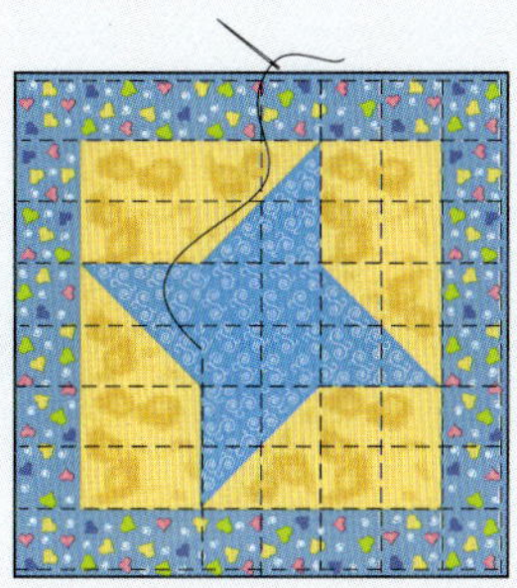

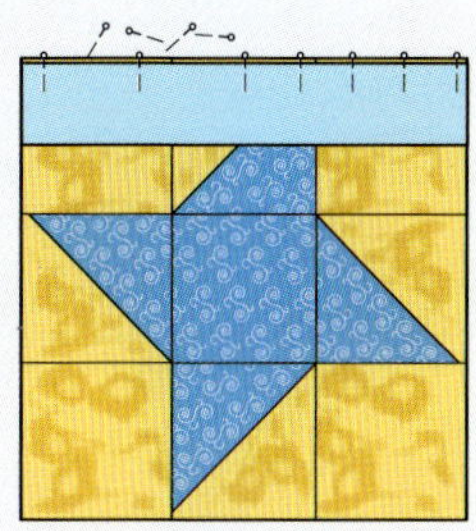

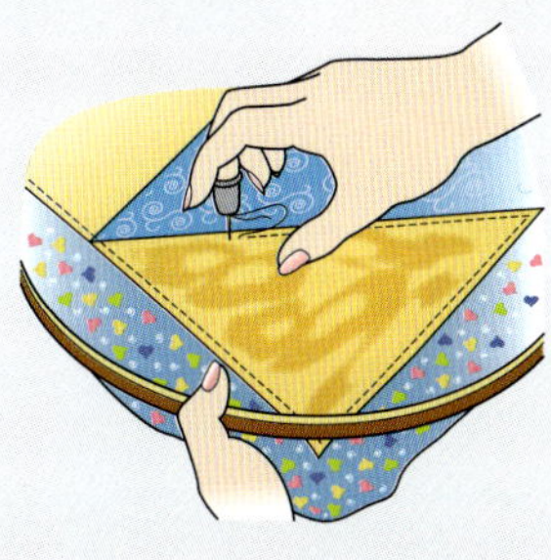

Materials

Patchwork fabrics

The easiest fabrics to work with for patchwork are closely woven, 100% cotton. They "cling" together making a stable unit for cutting and stitching, they don't fray too readily and they press well. Quilting shops and suppliers stock a fantastic range in both solid colours and prints, usually in 45 in/115 cm widths, and most of the quilts in this book are based on these cottons.

Backing and binding fabrics

The backing and binding fabrics should be the same type and weight as the fabrics used in the patchwork top. They can be a coordinating colour or a strong contrast. You could also be adventurous and piece the backing, too, to make a reversible quilt. In either case, the colour of the binding needs to work with both the top and the backing fabric designs.

Wadding or Batting

Various types of wadding are available in cotton, polyester, wool or mixed fibres. They can be bought in pre-cut sizes suitable for cot quilts and different sizes of bed quilts or in specific lengths cut from a bolt. They also come in different weights or "lofts" depending on how padded you want the quilt to be. Lightweight polyester wadding is the most commonly used, but some wool or cotton types are more suited to hand quilting. Some need to be closely quilted to prevent them from bunching up; others can be quilted up to 8 in/20 cm apart. Follow the manufacturer's instructions if in doubt.

Quantities

The quantities given at the beginning of each project have been calculated to allow for a bit extra – just in case! A few of the quilts combine cutting down the length of the fabric with cutting across the width. This is to make the most economical use of fabric or to obtain border pieces cut in one piece.

Unless otherwise stated, any 10 in/25 cm requirement is the "long" quarter – the full width of the fabric – and not the "fat" quarter, which is a piece 18 x 22 in/50 x 56 cm.

Preparation

All fabrics should be washed prior to use in order to wash out any excess dye and to avoid fabrics shrinking at different rates. Wash each fabric separately and rinse – repeatedly if necessary – until the water is clear of any colour run. If washing in a machine, cut a piece of white fabric from a larger piece. Place one piece in with the wash. After the wash, compare the white fabric with its other half. If they are the same, the fabric did not run. If a particular fabric continues to colour the water no matter how many times it is washed/rinsed and you have your heart set on using it, try washing it together with a small piece of each of the fabrics you intend to use with it. If these fabrics retain their original colours, i.e. they match the pieces not washed with the offending fabric, you would probably be safe in using it. But if in doubt – don't!

Once washed and before they are completely dry, iron the fabrics and fold them selvage to selvage – as they were originally on the bolt – in preparation for cutting. Be sure to fold them straight so that the selvages line up evenly, even if the cut edges are not parallel (this will be fixed later).

Threads

For machine quilting use lightweight or monofilament threads. For quilting by hand, use a thread labelled "quilting thread", which is heavier than normal sewing thread. Some threads are 100% cotton; others have a polyester core that is wrapped with cotton. You can use a thread either to match or to contrast with the fabric that is being quilted. Alternatively, use a variegated thread toning or contrasting with the patchwork. It is also acceptable to use several colours on the same piece of work. If the quilt is to be tied rather than quilted, use a heavier thread, such as coton perlé, coton à broder or stranded embroidery cotton.

Equipment

There are some essential pieces of equipment that have revolutionized the making of patchwork quilts. Rotary cutting equipment, consisting of a rotary cutter used with an acrylic ruler and self-healing cutting mat, has speeded up the process of cutting shapes and made it more accurate; the sewing machine makes assembling the patchwork and quilting the finished piece quick and easy.

Sewing machines

Evermore sophisticated, computerized machines are now available, but even a machine with just a straight stitch will speed up the process of assembling and quilting the patchwork considerably. Most sewing machines have a swing needle that allows the zig-zag stitching used for securing appliqué patches. Machines with decorative stitches provide the opportunity for additional embellishments.

Longarm quilting machines

These machines are used by professional quilters. You can choose from a huge library of quilting designs. There is also the option to have edge-to-edge quilting, all-over quilting of one design over the entire quilt, or a combination of patterns to complement each other. Alternatively, you can specify your own freehand style.

One of the advantages of this machine is that the quilt sandwich does not need to be tacked or pinned together prior to quilting: the pieced top, wadding and backing are mounted onto separate rollers that are part of the frame of the machine.

The machine is hand operated and takes considerable skill to work successfully. Most of the quilters who offer this quilting service advertize in patchwork magazines.

Rotary cutting

Rotary cutting has become the most commonly used method of cutting fabrics for patchwork. Most rotary cutting tools are available with either imperial or metric measurements.

ROTARY CUTTERS There are several different makes available, mainly in three different sizes: small, medium and large. The medium size (45 mm) is probably the one most widely used and perhaps the easiest to control. The smallest can be difficult to use with rulers. The largest is very useful when cutting through several layers of fabric but can take some practice to use. The rotary blade is extremely sharp, so always observe the safety instructions. It does become blunted with frequent use, so be sure to have replacement blades available.

ROTARY RULERS Various different rulers are available for use with rotary cutters. These are made of acrylic and are sufficiently thick to act as a guide for the rotary blade. You must use these rulers with the rotary cutter. Do not use metal rulers, as they will severely damage the blades.

The rulers are marked with measurements and angled lines used as a guide when cutting the fabrics. Ideally, these markings should be on the underside of the ruler, laser printed and easy to read. Angles should be marked in both directions. Different makes of rulers can have the lines printed in different colours. Choose one that you find easy on your eyes. Some makes also have a non-slip surface on the back – a very helpful addition.

The two most useful basic rulers are either a 24 x 6 in/60 x 15 cm, or one that is slightly shorter, and the small bias square ruler, 6½ in or 15 cm. This ruler is particularly useful for marking squares containing two triangles – the half-square triangle units. There are many other rulers designed for specific jobs that you can purchase if and when needed.

SELF-HEALING ROTARY CUTTING MATS These are essential companions to the rotary cutter and ruler. Do not attempt to cut on any other surface. The mats come in a number of different sizes and several different colours. The smaller ones are useful to take to classes, but for use at home, purchase the largest that you can afford and that suits your own workstation. There is usually a grid on one side, although both sides can be used. The lines on the mat are not always accurate, so it's better to use the lines on the ruler if possible.

Other useful equipment

Most other pieces of equipment are those that you will already have in your workbox. Those listed below are essential, but there is also a vast array of special tools devised by experienced quiltmakers that have specific uses. They are not needed by the beginner quilter but can really enhance the planning, cutting and quilting of your designs.

SCISSORS Two pairs are needed. One large pair of good-quality scissors should be used exclusively for cutting fabric. The second, smaller pair is for cutting paper, card or template plastic.

MARKERS Quilting designs can either be traced or drawn on the fabric prior to the layering or added after the layering with the aid of stencils or templates. Various marking tools are available: 2H pencils; silver, yellow or white pencils; fade away or washable marking pens; and Hera markers (which lightly indent the fabric). Whatever your choice, test the markers on a scrap of the fabric used in the quilt to ensure that the marks can be removed.

PINS Good-quality, clean, rustproof, straight pins are essential when a pin is required to hold the work in place for piecing. Flat-headed flower pins are useful because they don't add bulk.

SAFETY PINS These are useful for holding the quilt "sandwich" together for quilting, especially for those who prefer to machine quilt or want the speed of not tacking/basting the three layers together. Place the pins at regular intervals all over the surface.

NEEDLES For hand quilting, use "quilting" or "betweens" needles. Most quilters start with a no. 8 or 9 and progress to a no. 10 or 12. For machine stitching, the needles numbered 70/10 or 80/12 are both suitable for piecing and quilting. For tying with thicker thread, use a crewel or embroidery needle.

THIMBLES Two thimbles will be required for hand quilting. One thimble is worn on the hand pushing the needle and the other on the hand underneath the quilt "receiving" the needle. There are various types on the market ranging from metal to plastic to leather sheaths for the finger. There are also little patches that stick to the finger to protect it.

Hoops and frames

These are only needed if you are quilting by hand. They hold a section of the quilt under light tension to help you to achieve an even stitch. There are many types and sizes available, ranging from round and oval hoops to standing frames made of plastic pipes and wooden fixed frames.

Hoops are perhaps the easiest for a beginner. The 14 in/35 cm or 16 in/40 cm are best for portability. Many quilters continue to use hoops in preference to standing frames. When the quilt is in the hoop, the surface of the quilt should not be taut, as is the case with embroidery. If you place the quilt top with its hoop on a table, you should be able to push the fabric in the centre of the hoop with your finger and touch the table beneath. Without this "give", you will not be able to "rock" the needle for the quilting stitch. Do not leave the quilt in a hoop when you are not working on it, as the hoop will distort the fabrics.

Techniques

Rotary cutting

The basis of rotary cutting is that fabric is cut first in strips – usually across the width of the fabric, then cross-cut into squares or rectangles.

Making the edge straight

Before any accurate cutting can be done, first make sure the cut edge of the fabric is at right angles to the selvages.

1 Place the folded fabric on the cutting mat with the fabric smoothed out, the selvages exactly aligned at the top and the bulk of the fabric on the side that is not your cutting hand. Place the ruler on the fabric next to the cut edge, aligning the horizontal lines on the ruler with the fold and with the selvages.

2 Place your non-cutting hand on the ruler to hold it straight and apply pressure. Keep the hand holding the ruler in line with the cutting hand. Place the cutter on the mat just below the fabric and up against the ruler. Start cutting by running the cutter upwards and next to the edge of the ruler (diagram 1).

3 When the cutter becomes level with your extended fingertips, stop cutting but leave the cutter in position and carefully move the hand holding the ruler further along the ruler to keep the applied pressure in the area where the cutting is taking place. Continue cutting and moving the steadying hand as necessary until you have cut completely across the fabric. As soon as the cut is complete, close the safety shield on the cutter. If you run out of cutting mat, you will need to reposition the fabric, but this is not ideal as it can bring the fabric out of alignment.

4 Open out the narrow strip of fabric just cut off. Check to make sure that a "valley" or a "hill" has not appeared at the point of the fold on the edge just cut; it should be perfectly straight. If it is not, the fabric was not folded correctly. Fold the fabric again, making sure that this time the selvages are exactly aligned. Make another cut to straighten the edge and check again.

Cutting strips

The next stage is to cut strips across the width of the fabric. To do this, change the position of the fabric to the opposite side of the board, then use the measurements on the ruler to cut the strips.

1 Place the fabric on the cutting mat on the side of your cutting hand. Place the ruler on the mat so that it overlaps the fabric. Align the cut edge of the fabric with the vertical line on the ruler that corresponds to the measurement that you wish to cut. The horizontal lines on the ruler should be aligned with the folded edge and the selvage of the fabric.

2 As before, place one hand on the ruler to apply pressure while cutting the fabric with the other hand (diagram 2).

1

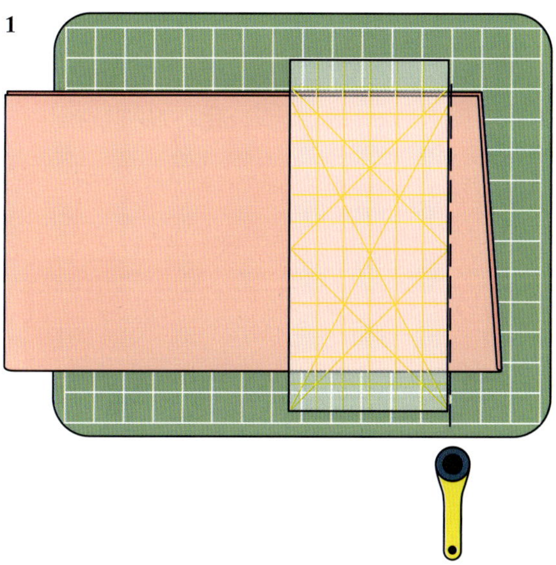

2

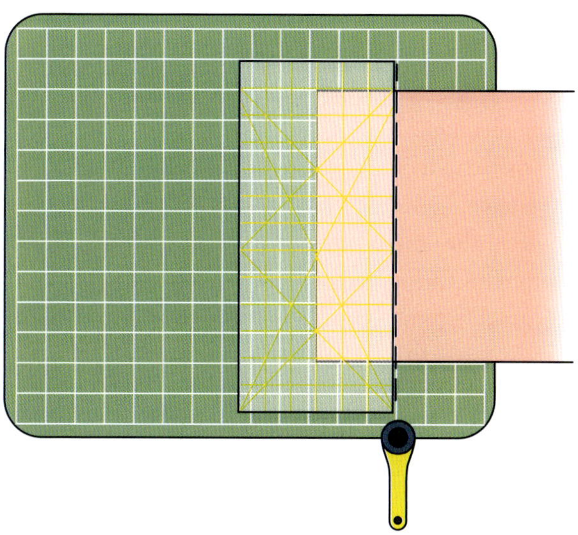

Cross-cutting

The strips can now be cut into smaller units, described as cross-cutting, and these units are sometimes sub-cut into triangles.

SQUARES

1 Place the strip just cut on the cutting mat with the longest edge horizontal to you and most of the fabric on the side of the non-cutting hand. Cut off the selvages in the same way in which you straightened the fabric edge at the start of the process.

2 Now place the strip on the opposite side of the mat and cut across (cross-cut) the strip using the same measurement on the rule as used for cutting the strip; ensure that the horizontal lines of the ruler align with the horizontal edge of the fabric. You have now created two squares of the required measurement (diagram 3). Repeat as required.

3

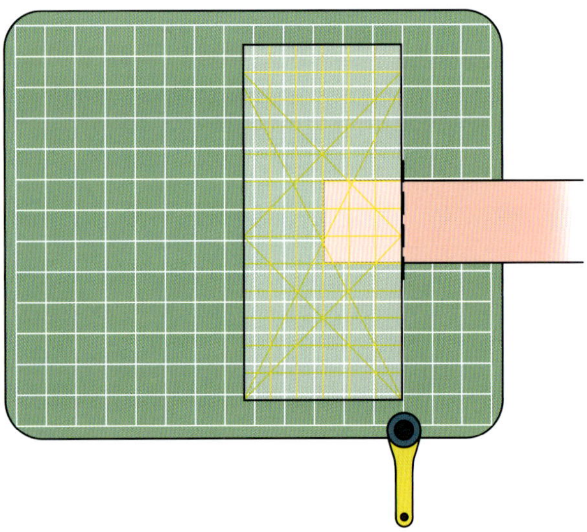

RECTANGLES

1 First cut a strip to one of the required side measurements for the rectangle. Remove the selvages.

2 Turn the strip to the horizontal position as for the squares.

3 Cross-cut this strip using the other side measurement required for the rectangle. Again, ensure that the horizontal lines of the ruler align with the horizontal cut edges of the strip.

WIDE STRIPS

Placing two rulers side by side can aid the cutting of extra-wide strips. If you don't have two rulers, place the fabric on the cutting mat in the correct position for cutting. Align the cut edge of the fabric with one of the vertical lines running completely across the cutting board, and the folded edge with one of the horizontal lines. If the measurement does not fall on one of the lines on the cutting mat, use the ruler in conjunction with the cutting mat.

MULTI-STRIP UNITS

This two-stage method of cutting strips, then cross-cutting into squares or rectangles, can also be used to speed up the cutting of multi-strip units to provide strip blocks.

1 Cut the required number and size of strips and stitch together as per the instructions for the block/quilt you are making. Press the seams and check that they are smooth on the right side of the strip unit with no pleats or wrinkles.

2 Place the unit right side up in the horizontal position on the cutting mat. Align the horizontal lines on the ruler with the longer cut edges of the strips and with the seam lines just created (diagram 4). If, after you have cut a few cross-cuts, the lines on the ruler do not line up with the cut edges as well as the seam lines, re-cut the end to straighten it before cutting any more units.

4

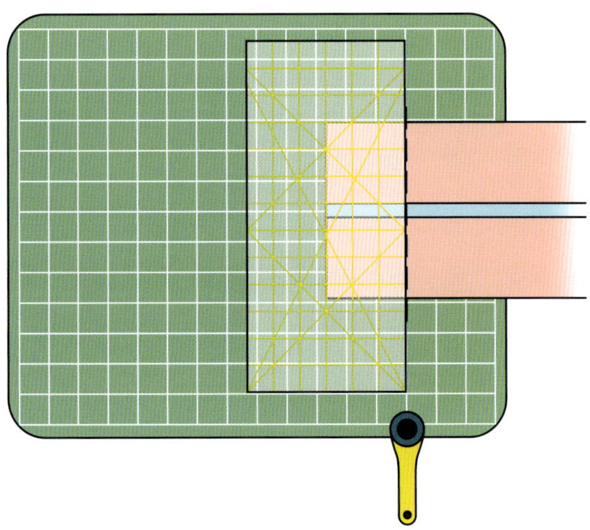

Rotary cutting triangles

Squares can be divided into either two or four triangles, called half-square or quarter-square triangles. Both sizes of triangle can be quickly cut using the rotary cutter or they can be made even faster by a quick piecing method described on pages 16 to 17.

CUTTING HALF-SQUARE TRIANGLES

1 Cut the fabric into strips of the correct depth and remove the selvages. Cross-cut the strips into squares of the correct width.

2 Align the 45° angle line on the ruler with the sides of the square and place the edge of the ruler so that it goes diagonally across the square from corner to corner. Cut the square on this diagonal, creating two half-square triangles (diagram 5).

CUTTING QUARTER-SQUARE TRIANGLES

1 Cut the fabric into strips of the correct depth and remove the selvages.

2 Cross-cut the strips into squares of the correct width. Cut the square into two half-square triangles, as before.

3 You can either repeat this procedure on the other diagonal (diagram 6) or, if you are wary of the fabric slipping now that it is in two pieces, separate the two triangles and cut them individually. Align one of the horizontal lines of the ruler with the long edge of the triangle, the 45° line with the short edge of the triangle and the edge of the ruler placed on the point of the triangle opposite the long edge. Cut this half-square triangle into two quarter-square triangles.

5

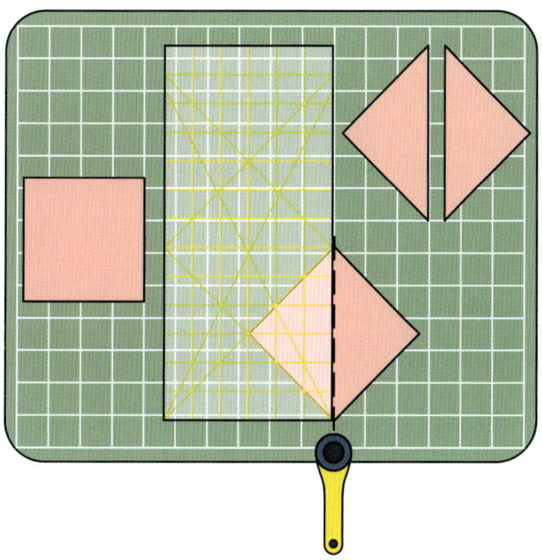

6

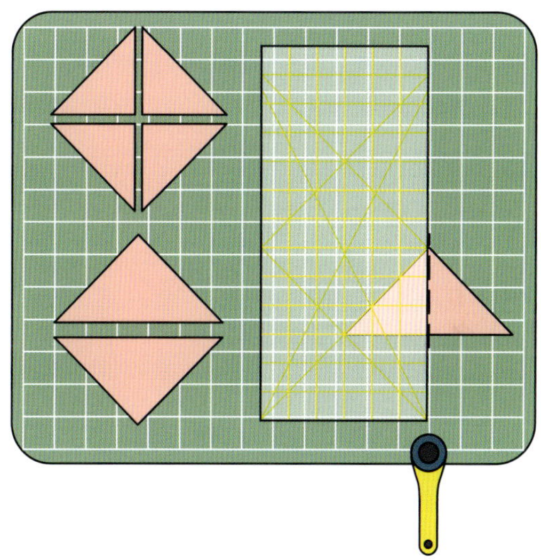

Seams

To stitch accurately, you must be able to use the correct seam allowance without having to mark it on the fabric. To do this, you use the foot or the bed of your sewing machine as a guide. Many machines today have a "¼ in" or "patchwork" foot available as an extra. There are also various generic foot accessories available that will fit most machines. Before you start any piecing, check that you can make this seam allowance accurately.

CHECKING THE MACHINE FOR THE CORRECT SEAM ALLOWANCE

Unthread the machine. Place a piece of paper under the presser foot, so that the right-hand edge of the paper aligns with the right-hand edge of the presser foot. Stitch a seam line on the paper. A row of holes will appear. Remove the paper from the machine and measure the distance from the holes to the edge of the paper. If it is not the correct width, i.e. ¼ in/0.75 cm, try one of the following:

1. If your machine has a number of different needle positions, try moving the needle in the direction required to make the seam allowance accurate and stitch a row again.
2. Draw a line on the paper to the correct seam allowance, i.e. ¼ in/0.75 cm from the edge of the paper. Place the paper under the presser foot, aligning the drawn line with the needle. Lower the presser foot to hold the paper securely and, to double-check, lower the needle to ensure that it is directly on top of the drawn line.

   Fix a piece of masking tape on the bed of the machine so that the left-hand edge of the tape lines up with the right-hand edge of the paper. This can also be done with magnetic strips available on the market to be used as seam guides. But do take advice on using these if your machine is computerized or electronic.

STITCHING ¼ IN/0.75 CM SEAMS

When stitching pieces together, line up the edge of the fabric with the right-hand edge of the presser foot or with the left-hand edge of the tape or the magnetic strip on the bed of your machine, if you have used this method.

CHECKING THE FABRIC FOR THE CORRECT SEAM ALLOWANCE

As so much of the success of a patchwork depends on accuracy of cutting and seaming, it is worth double-checking on the fabric that you are stitching a ¼ in/0.75 cm seam.

Cut three strips of fabric 1½ in/4 cm wide. Stitch these together along the long edges. Press the seams away from the centre strip. Measure the centre strip. It should measure exactly 1 in/2.5 cm wide. If not, reposition the needle/tape and try again.

STITCH LENGTH

The stitch length used is normally 12 stitches to the inch or 5 to the centimetre. If the pieces being stitched together are to be cross-cut into smaller units, it is advisable to slightly shorten the stitch, which will mean the seam is less likely to unravel. It is also good practice to start each new project with a new needle in a clean machine – free of fluff around the bobbin housing.

Quick machine piecing

The three most basic techniques are for stitching pairs of patches together (chain piecing), for stitching half-square triangle units and for stitching quarter-square triangle units.

CHAIN PIECING

Have all the pairs of patches or strips together ready in a pile. Place the first two patches or strips in the machine, right sides together, and stitch them together. Just before reaching the end, stop stitching and pick up the next two patches or strips. Place them on the bed of the machine, so that they just touch the patches under the needle. Stitch off one set and onto the next. Repeat this process until all the pairs are stitched to create a "chain" of pieced patches/strips (diagram 7). Cut the thread between each unit to separate them. Open out and press the seams according to the instructions given with each project.

7

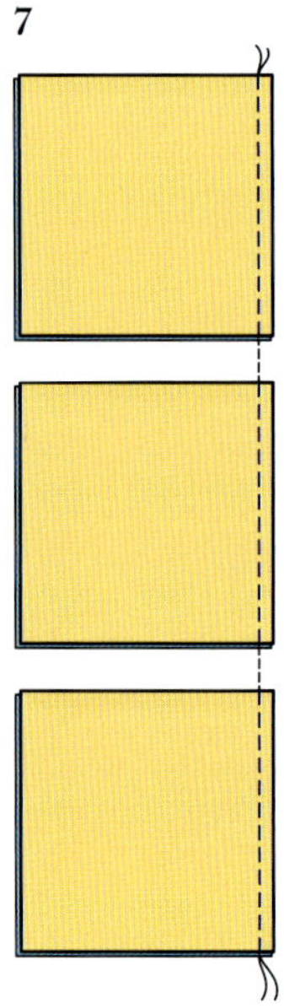

STITCHING HALF-SQUARE TRIANGLE UNITS

This is a quick method of creating a bi-coloured square without cutting the triangles first.

1 Cut two squares of different coloured fabrics to the correct measurement, i.e. the finished size of the bi-coloured square plus ⅝ in/1.75 cm. Place them right sides together, aligning all raw edges. On the wrong side of the top square, draw a diagonal line from one corner to the other.

2 Stitch ¼ in/0.75 cm away on either side of the drawn line (diagram 8).

8

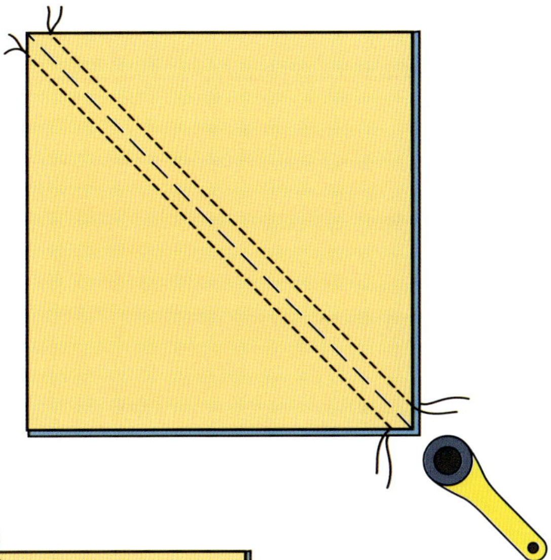

9

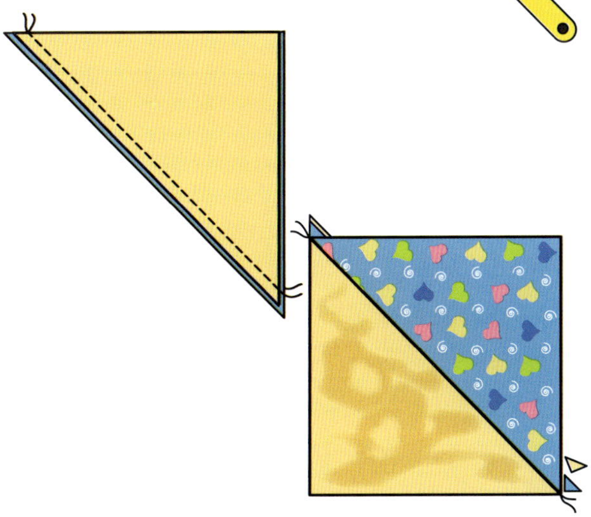

3 Cut the two halves apart by cutting on the drawn line. Open out and press the seams according to the instructions given with each project. You now have two squares, each containing two triangles. Trim off the corners (diagram 9).

STITCHING QUARTER-SQUARE TRIANGLE UNITS

This method also creates triangles from squares without first cutting the triangles.

1 Cut squares to the finished size of a square containing four triangles plus 1¼ in/3.5 cm. Follow the stitching, cutting apart and pressing sequence as for the half-square triangles units.

2 Place the two bi-coloured squares right sides together. Ensure that each triangle is facing a triangle of a different colour. Draw a line diagonally from corner to corner, at right angles to the stitched seam.

3 Pin carefully to match the seams, then stitch ¼ in/0.75 cm away on either side of the line. Before cutting apart, open up each side and check to see that the points match in the centre (diagram 10).

10

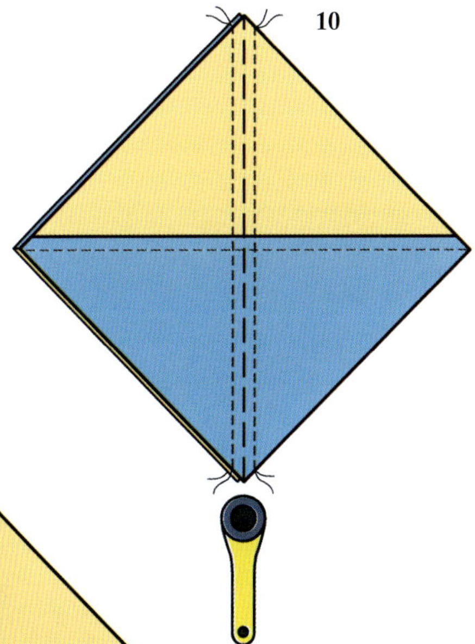

11

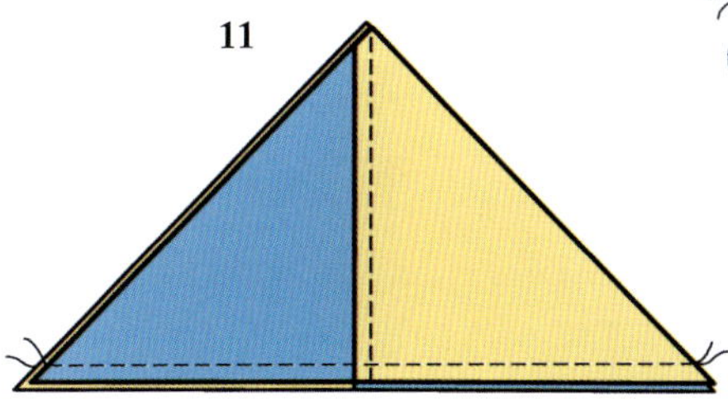

4 Cut apart on the drawn line. You now have two squares, each containing four triangles (diagram 11).

Pressing

Each project will have instructions on the direction in which to press the seam allowances. These have been designed to facilitate easier piecing at junctions and to reduce the bulk so that seam allowances do not lay one on top of the other. Pressing as you complete each stage of the piecing will also improve the accuracy and look of your work. Take care not to distort the patches. Be gentle, not fierce, with the iron.

Adding the borders

Most patchwork tops are framed by one or more borders. The simplest way of adding borders is to add strips first to the top and bottom of the quilt and then to the sides, producing abutted corners. A more complicated method is to add strips to adjacent sides and join them with seams at 45 degrees, giving mitred borders. Only the first method is used for the quilts in this book.

ADDING BORDERS WITH ABUTTED CORNERS

The measurements for the borders required for each quilt in the book will be given in the instructions. However, it is always wise to measure your own work to determine the actual measurement.

1 Measure the quilt through the centre across the width edge to edge. Cut the strips for the top and bottom borders to this length by the width specified for the border.

12

2 Pin the strips to the quilt by pinning first at each end, then in the middle, then evenly spaced along the edge. By pinning in this manner, it is possible to ensure that the quilt "fits" the border. Stitch the border strips into position on the top and bottom edge of the quilt (diagram 12). Press the seams towards the border.

3 Measure the quilt through the centre from top to bottom. Cut the side border strips to this measurement.

4 Pin and stitch the borders to each side of the quilt as before (diagram 13). Press the seams towards the border.

13

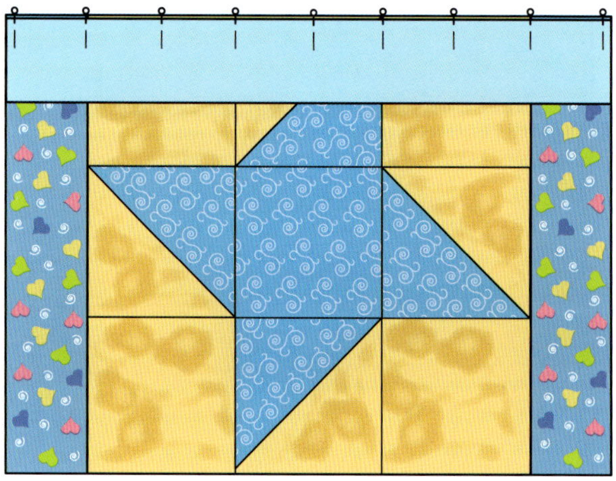

Quilting

The three layers or "sandwich" of the backing/wadding/pieced top are held together by quilting or by tying. The quilting can be done by hand or machine. The tying is done by hand stitching decorative ties at strategic points on the quilt. Buttons can also be used for the same purpose.

LAYERING/SANDWICHING

Prior to any quilting, unless you are using a longarm quilting machine, the pieced top must be layered with the wadding and the backing. The wadding and the backing should be slightly larger than the quilt top – approximately 2 in/5 cm on all sides. There are two different methods for assembling the three layers depending on whether the quilts has bound edges or not.

ASSEMBLING PRIOR TO BINDING

1 Lay out the backing fabric wrong side uppermost. Ensure that it is stretched out and smooth. Secure the edges with masking tape at intervals along the edges to help to hold it in position.

2 Place the wadding on top of the backing fabric. If you need to join two pieces of wadding first, butt the edges and stitch together by hand using a herringbone stitch (diagram 14).

3 Place the pieced top right side up and centred on top of the wadding.

14

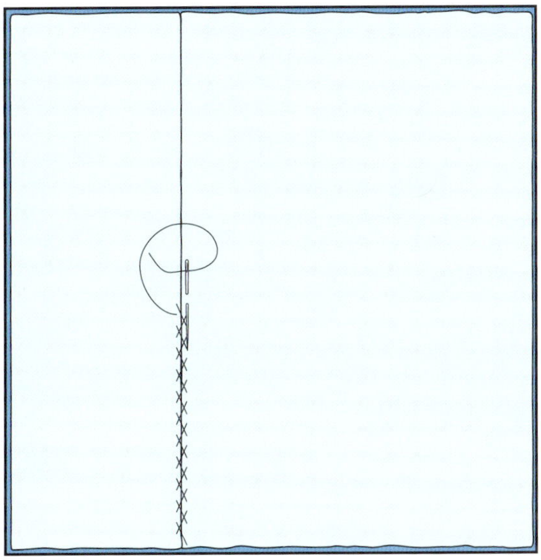

ASSEMBLING WHERE NO BINDING IS USED ("BAGGING OUT")

1 Spread out the wadding on a flat surface. Smooth out to ensure there are no wrinkles.

2 Place the backing fabric centrally on top of the wadding, right side uppermost.

3 Place the pieced top centrally over the backing, wrong side uppermost. Pin with straight pins around the edges to keep them together.

4 Stitch around all four sides with a ¼ in/0.75 cm seam allowance but leaving an opening of about 15–18 in/35–45 cm in one of the sides.

5 Trim the excess wadding and backing at the sides and across the corners to reduce bulk, then turn the quilt right side out, so that the wadding is in the middle. Slip-stitch the opening closed.

6 Smooth out the layers of the quilt and roll and finger-press the edges so that the seam lies along the edge or just underneath.

BASTING PRIOR TO QUILTING

If the piece is to be quilted rather than tied, the three layers now need to be held together at regular intervals. This can be done by basting or by using safety pins. For either method, start in the centre of the quilt and work out to the edges.

Using a long length of thread, start basting in the centre of the quilt top. Only pull about half of the thread through as you start stitching. Once you have reached the edge, go back and thread the other end of the thread and baste to the opposite edge. Repeat this process, stitching in a grid of horizontal and vertical lines over the whole quilt top (diagram 15).

15

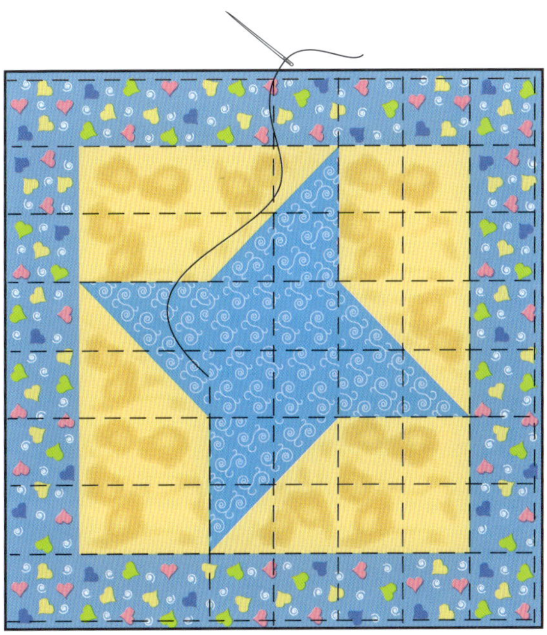

Machine Quilting

Designs to be used for machine quilting should ideally be those that have one continuous line. The lines can be straight or free- form curves and squiggles. For either type, be sure to keep the density of stitching the same. With either method, continuous lines of stitching will be visible both on the top and on the back of the quilt. It is a quick method but requires careful preparation.

There is a wide variety of tools available designed to help make handling the quilt easier during the machine quilting process. However, the most essential requirement is practice.

It is worth making up a practice sandwich – if possible using the same fabrics and wadding as used in the actual quilt – to be sure that you get the effect you want. In any case, plan the quilting design first, otherwise there is a danger that you will start with quite dense stitching, then tire of the process and begin to space out the lines, producing an uneven pattern.

When starting and stopping the stitching during machine quilting, either reduce the stitch length to zero or stitch several stitches in one spot. If you do not like the build-up of stitches that this method produces, leave long tails on the thread when you start and stop. Later, pull these threads through to one side of the quilt, knot them, then thread them into a needle. Push the needle into the fabric and into the wadding, but not through to the other side of the quilt, and then back out through the fabric again about 1 in/2.5 cm away from where the needle entered the quilt. Cut off the excess thread.

IN-THE-DITCH MACHINE QUILTING

One of the easiest and most common forms of straight line quilting is called "in-the-ditch" and involves stitching just beside a seam line on the side without the seam allowances. Some machines require a walking foot to stitch the three layers together. These are used with the feed dogs up and, while in use, the machine controls the direction and stitch length.

FREE MOTION MACHINE QUILTING

When machine quilting in freehand, a darning foot is used with the feed dogs down, so that you can move the quilt forwards, backwards and sideways. This is easier on some machines than others, but all require a bit of practice.

Hand Quilting

The stitch used for hand quilting is a running stitch. The needle goes into the quilt through to the back and returns to the top of the quilt all in one movement. The aim is to have the size of the stitches and spaces between them the same.

1 Thread a needle with an 18 in/45 cm length of quilting thread and knot the end. Push the needle into the fabric and into the wadding, but not through to the back, about 1 in/2.5 cm away from where you want to start stitching. Bring the needle up through the fabric at the point where you will begin stitching. Gently pull on the thread to "pop" the knot through into the wadding.

2 To make a perfect quilting stitch, the needle needs to enter the fabric perpendicular to the quilt top. Holding the needle between your first finger and thumb, push the needle into the fabric until it hits the thimble on the finger of the hand underneath.

3 The needle can now be held between the thimble on your sewing hand and the thimble on the finger underneath. Release your thumb and first finger hold on the needle. Place your thumb on the quilt top just in front of where the needle will come back up to the top and gently press down on the quilt (diagram 16).

4 At the same time, rock the thread end of the needle down towards the quilt top and push the needle up from

16

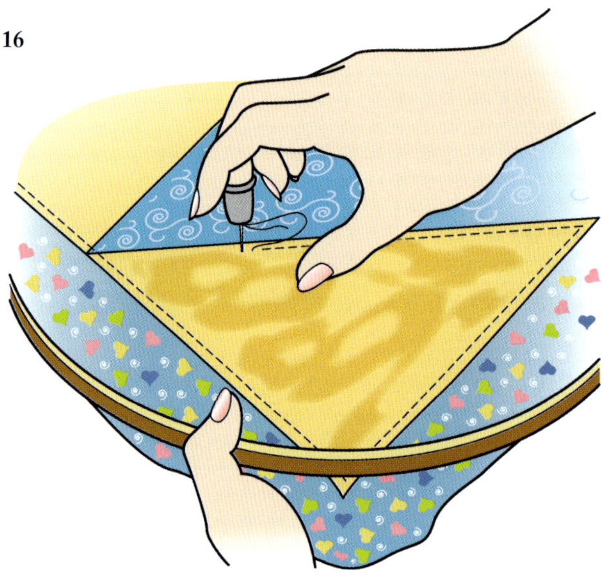

underneath so that the point appears on the top of the quilt. You can either pull the needle through now, making only one stitch, or rock the needle up to the vertical again, push the needle through to the back, then rock the needle up to the quilt top, again placing another stitch on the needle. Repeat until you can no longer rock the needle into a completely upright position (diagram 17). Pull the needle through the quilt. One stitch at a time or several placed on the needle at once – "the rocking stitch" – before pulling the thread through, are both acceptable.

17

5 When the stitching is complete, tie a knot in the thread close to the quilt surface. Push the needle into the quilt top and the wadding next to the knot, but not through to the back of the quilt. Bring the needle up again about 1 in/2.5 cm away and gently tug on the thread to "pop" the knot through the fabric and into the wadding. Cut the thread.

Binding

Once the quilting is completed, the quilt is usually (but not always) finished off with a binding to enclose the raw edges. This binding can be cut on the straight or on the bias. Either way, the binding is usually best done with a double fold. It can be applied in four separate pieces to each of the four sides, or the binding strips can be joined together and stitched to the quilt in one continuous strip with mitred corners. To join straight-cut pieces for a continuous strip, use straight seams; to join bias-cut pieces, use diagonal seams (diagram 18).

18

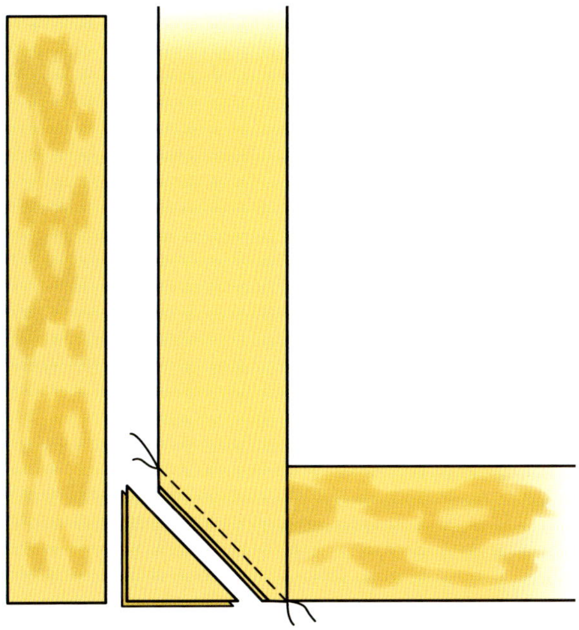

For either method, the width of the bias strips should be cut to the following measurement: finished binding width x four + the seam allowance x two.
For example:
A finished binding width of ½ in would be cut as 2½ in:
(½ in x 4) + (¼ in x 2) = 2½ in
or 1.25 cm would be cut 6.5 cm:
(1.25 cm x 4) + (0.75 cm x 2) = 6.5 cm

the Projects

Charm Square Bag

DESIGNED BY SUE WARREN

A great way to use commercially produced Charm Squares or break into your stash and make your own.

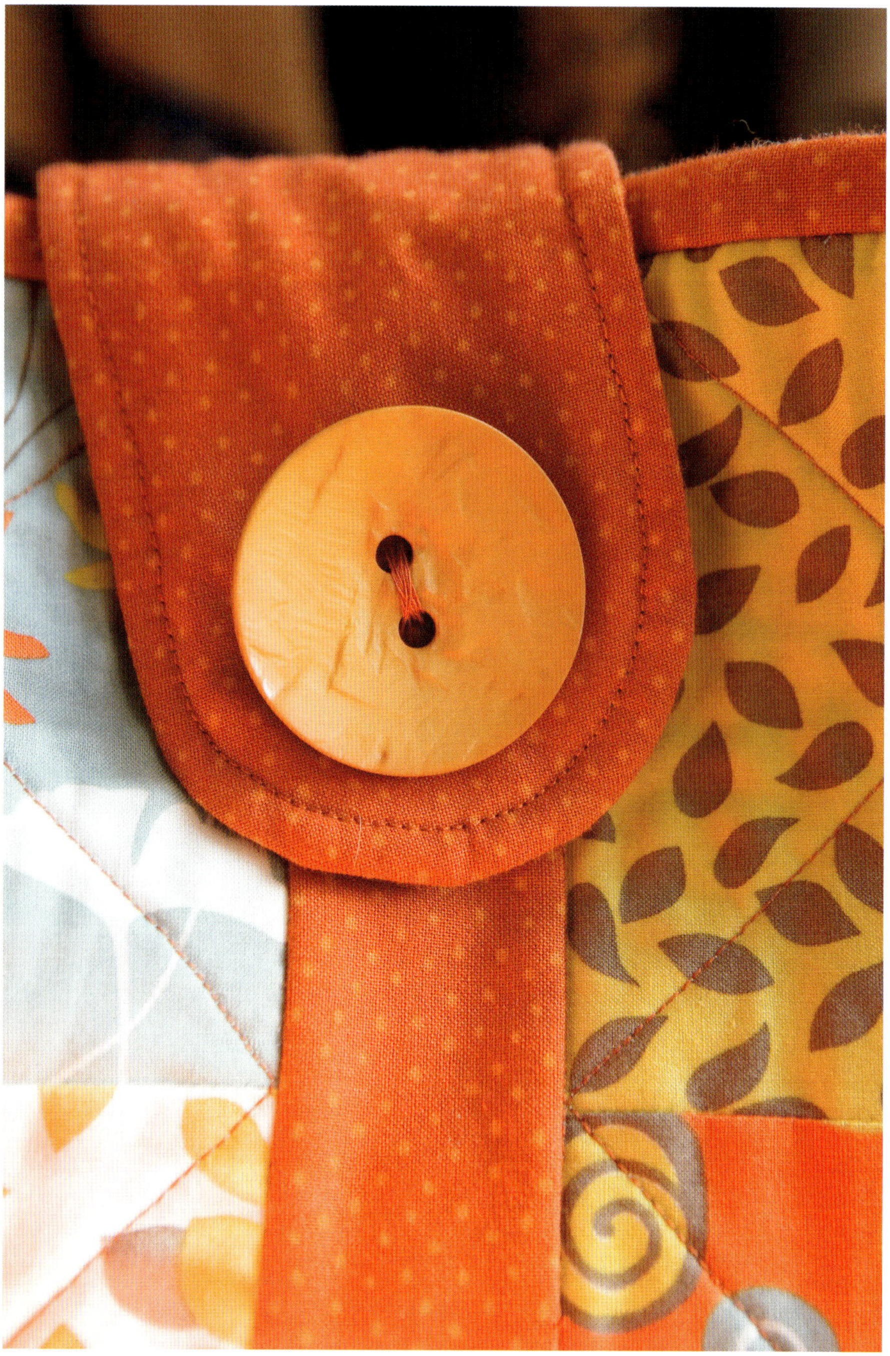

FINISHED SIZE
Approximately 23 x 17½ in/58.5 x 44.5 cm

YOU WILL NEED
All fabrics are 100% cotton

- **Body of quilt** 32 squares 5 in/12.75 cm for bag

  Four squares 5 in/12.75 cm for inner pocket

- **Sashing strips, handles, tab and binding** Contrast fabric, ⅝ yd/60 cm

- **Lining** ¾ yd/70 cm

- **Wadding** Two pieces 20 x 26 in/50 x 65 cm

  Two pieces 20 x ½ in/ 50 x 1.25 cm

  Piece approximately 7 x 4½ in/18 x 11.5 cm for tab

- **Accessories** ½ in/1.25 cm magnetic closure

  Large button

CUTTING

Contrast fabric Cut eight strips 2 x 18½ in/5 x 47 cm.
Handles Cut one strip 3½ in/9 cm wide x width of the fabric.
Binding Cut one strip 2½ in/6.5 cm wide x width of the fabric.
Lining Fabric Cut two pieces 24½ x 18½ in/62.25 x 47 cm.

STITCHING

1. Make eight strip sets of four squares. Press all the seams in one direction.
2. Stitch the square sets with a contrast strip to the right of each set. Press toward the contrast strip (diagram **A**).

A

3. Pin/tack each panel to a piece of flat wadding. Quilt in the ditch either side of the contrast strips and on the diagonal of each square. Trim away excess wadding.
4. With right sides together stitch the side seams to form a continuous length of alternating squares and contrast strips. Then sew the bottom edge, making sure that the contrast strips match and that there is a contrast strip on each side to form side seam.
5. To square off the bottom of the bag line up the bottom seam with the side contrast strip. Sew 2½ in/6.5 cm from the point created by the fold (diagram **B**).
6. On the wrong side measure 1½ in/4 cm in from the side edge and stitch a short seam 2½ in/6.5 cm down from the top edge. Back stitch ends (diagram **C**).
7. Insert one half of a magnetic closure in the centre front contrast strip, 2 in/5 cm from the top of the bag.

B

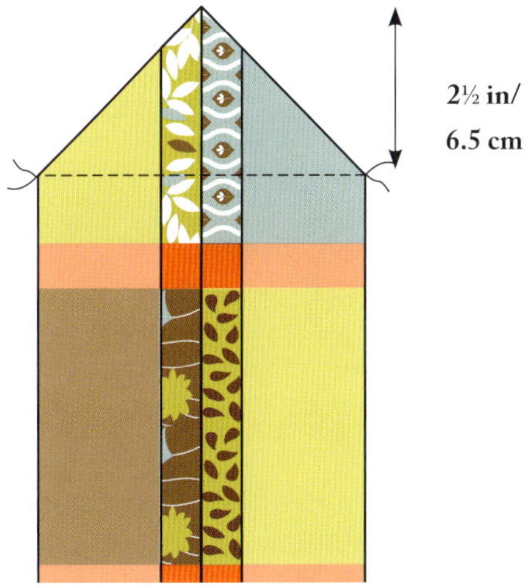

C

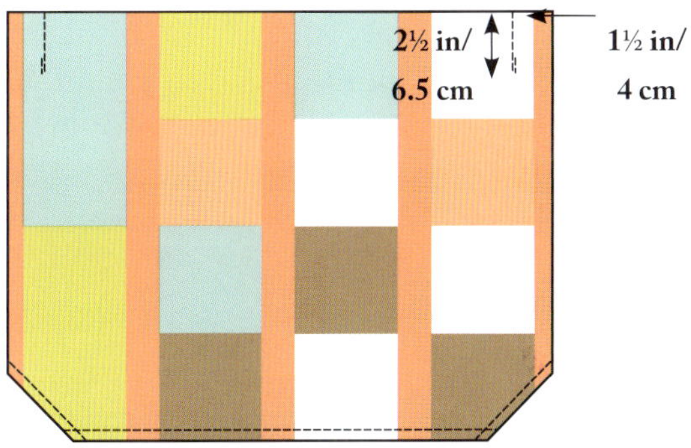

8. To make the pocket stitch four squares together to make a four-patch. Fold in half with right sides together, stitch along short edges. Turn through to right side and press. With right sides together position raw edge of the pocket 10 in/25.5 cm from the bottom edge of the lining and stitch using a scant ¼ in/0.75 cm. Flip the

pocket up to conceal the seam, top stitch down each side and bottom edge of the pocket. Stitch in the centre between the squares to make two pockets (diagram **D**).

D

9 Make up lining in the same way as the bag by following steps 4–6.

10 Insert the lining into the bag, wrong sides together. Ease, if necessary, and pin top edges of bag and lining together.

11 Fold and press under ¼ in/0.75 cm on both long sides of the handle strips. Place a wadding strip under one of the pressed edges and fold the whole strip in half to encase the wadding. Stitch ⅛ in/0.25 cm from each long edge, then stitch another two or three rows along the length of the handles (a machine decorative stitch could be used). Trim handles to the desired length approx 20 in/50 cm and pin to the outside of the bag. Line up the handles with the contrast strips on the front and back of the bag (diagram **E**).

E

12 From the tab template cut two tabs from contrast fabric and one from wadding. Lay one of the fabric tabs on top of the wadding. Right side facing and insert the second half of the magnetic closure. Position the second tab on top of the first right sides together and stitch as shown on the template on the right.

13 Trim the seam, clip the curved edges and turn right side out. Top stitch ¼ in/0.75 cm from edge. Pin the tab to the centre back of the bag with raw edges together and leave the tab hanging down.

14 Increase the stitch length on the sewing machine and use a scant ¼ in/0.75 cm seam to tack around the top edge of the bag. This will hold the lining, handles and tab in position ready for binding.

15 Fold the 2½ in/6.5 cm binding in half along its length and press. With right sides together and starting at the centre, back stitch the binding around the top of the bag. Fold the binding to the wrong side and slip-stitch to the inside of the bag.

16 To stabilise the bag, cut a piece of firm card to the size of the base, cover with some left over lining (a glue stick will hold the fabric in place) and put inside the bottom of the bag.

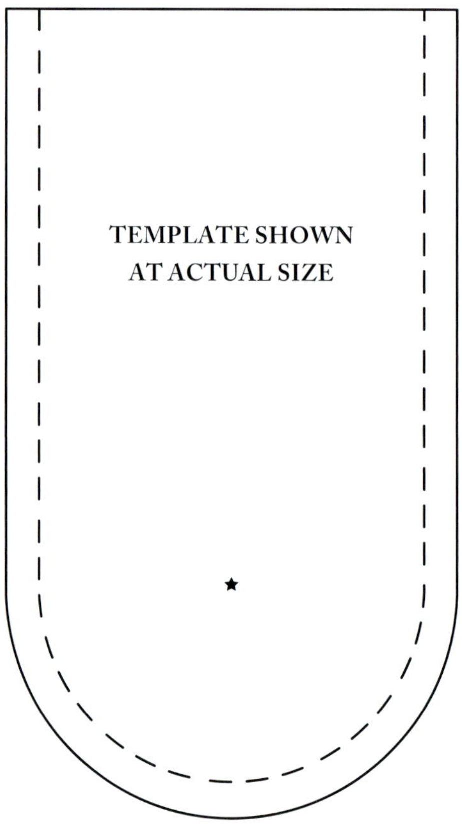

LOOKED AT ANOTHER WAY

Make the bag to suit your mood or just choose two or three fabrics for a more controlled colourway. This project would make a great gift for friends of family so why not make several in every colourway!

Water's Edge

DESIGNED BY MARION PATTERSON

This simple pattern based on halved layer cakes can be put together very quickly but is still attractive and especially good at showing off the beauty of the fabric itself. Water's Edge, coincidentally, was the range of Moda Layer Cake used for this pattern of quilt.

FINISHED SIZE
45½ x 70 in/116 x 178 cm

YOU WILL NEED
All fabrics are 100% cotton

- **Body of quilt** One layer cake packet or 40 different 10 in/25.5 cm squares
- **Backing** If you are using a fabric that is 45 in/114 cm or more wide you will need 2¼ yds/2 mtrs or you will need to join the backing to give you a width of 4½ yds/4 mtrs
- **Binding** Coordinating colour fabric, 18 in/45 cm
- **Wadding** 50 x 76 in/127 x 193 cm

QUILT PLAN

CUTTING

1. This quilt is made up of 25 blocks. Take the 40 x 10 in/25.5 cm squares and cut in half to give you 80 rectangles, 5 x 10 in/12.75 x 25.5 cm. Keep the cut squares in order in two piles (diagram **A**).
2. If you are not using a layer cake, cut 40 squares, 10 x 10 in/25.5 x 25.5 cm from your chosen fabrics and then cut in half to give you 80 rectangles, 5 x 10 in/12.75 x 25.5 cm. Keep the cut squares in order in two piles (diagram **A**).
3. From the binding fabric cut seven strips, 2¼ in/5.5 cm wide, across the width of the fabric.

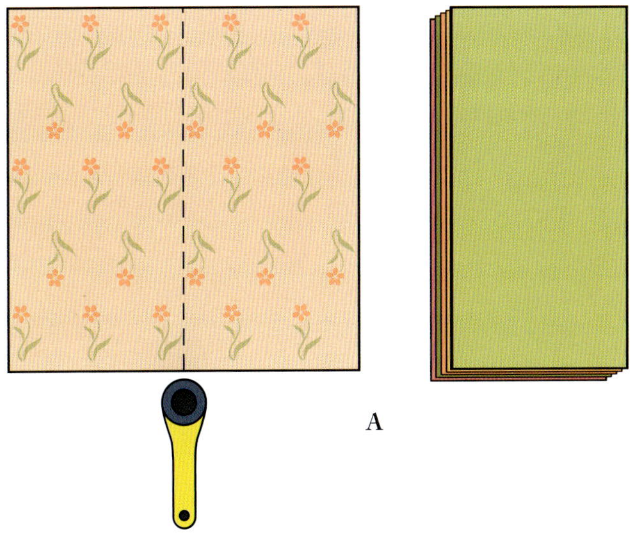
A

B

C

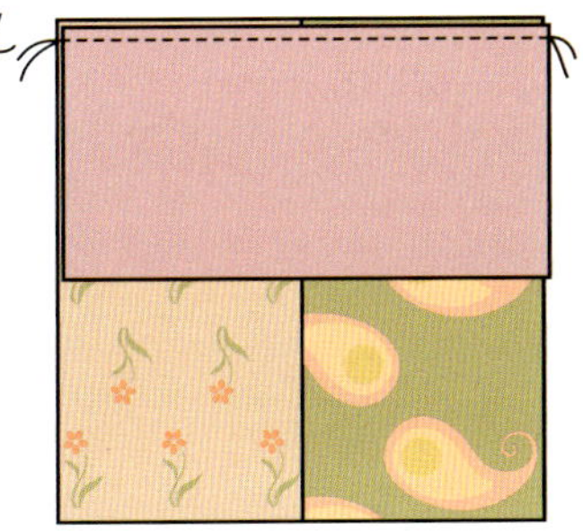
D

STITCHING

1. You now have two piles of rectangles. Take the top 10 rectangles from one pile and set aside. Turn one pile over so that the top fabric becomes the bottom fabric. The two piles of fabric will now have one with the right side facing up and one with the wrong side facing up (diagram **B**).
2. Take one rectangle from each pile. With right sides facing, join them together using a ¼ in/0.75 cm seam allowance. Repeat this until you have joined together 25 blocks (diagram **C**). Press the seams to one side. Alternatively, you can sort through the two piles of rectangles and pair them up as desired.
3. You will now have 20 rectangles left. Add the 10 you set aside to this pile. Cut ½ in/1.25 cm off the length to make 5 x 9½ in/12.75 x 24 cm rectangles. Join these rectangles on to the top edge of each previously pieced block. This will give you a block measuring 9½ x 14¼ in/24 x 37 cm (diagram **D**).
4. The quilt top is made up of five blocks across by five rows down. Take five of the blocks and join them in a row – do this five times. Then join the five rows together.

E

FINISHING

1 Measure the quilt top through the centre horizontally and vertically to check your measurements. The quilt top should measure 45½ x 70 in/116 x 178 cm. If the measurements are different from this adjust your wadding and backing fabric to fit.

2 If the backing fabric is not wide enough to fit the quilt top, join the fabric to make one piece measuring at least 50 x 76 in/127 x 193 cm taking a ½ in/1.25 cm seam allowance. Press the seam open.

3 Spread the backing right side down on a flat surface making sure that you smooth out any wrinkles then add the wadding and the pieced top, right side up on top. Baste the layers together with safety pins, tack with a tacking gun or hand baste in a grid (diagram **E**).

4 Hand or machine stitch the quilt. Join all the binding strips into one length and use to bind the quilt with a double-fold binding, mitred at the corners.

NOTE If you purchase the wadding in a pack, it is advisable to unpack it and hang it somewhere to allow the creases to drop for 24 hours. Alternatively, open out the wadding and pop it into a tumble dryer on a cool setting for about 10 minutes. Wadding purchased off the roll by the yard/meter does not usually need to be hung and is ready to use.

LOOKED AT ANOTHER WAY

You can make this quilt using large scraps of fabrics. For example if you don't have 10 in/ 25.5 cm squares but have lots of 5 x 10 in/12.75 x 25.5 cm pieces, then cut your rectangles from them and make this a scrap quilt. Alternatively, you can use a minimum of three different fabrics in one colour way and this will give you a more uniform look.

Fan Quilt

DESIGNED BY SALLY ABLETT

This quilt is a great way of displaying all those 1930s style fabrics you've been wanting to use and the multi layered effect of the design gives it real depth. There is only one block involved so it couldn't be easier.

FINISHED SIZE
56 in/142.25 cm square

YOU WILL NEED
All fabrics are 100% cotton

- **Body of quilt** Background fabric: 2⅞ yds/2.65 mtrs
- 18 fat quarters of 1930s style fabrics
- Green fabric for borders and binding: 1¼ yd/1 mtr
- **Backing** 64 in/163 cm square
- **Wadding** 64 in/163 cm square

QUILT PLAN

CUTTING

Background fabric

36 squares measuring 8½ in/22 cm.

5 squares measuring 9¼ in/23.5 cm cut in half diagonally twice for border.

4 squares measuring 4⅞ in/12.5 cm cut in half diagonally once for borders.

Green border and binding fabric

6 squares measuring 9¼ in/23.5 cm cut in half diagonally twice for border.

4 squares measuring 4½ in/11.5 cm for border.

6 strips measuring 2¼ in/5.5 cm across width of fabric.

Fans

216 pieces from template A.

36 pieces from template B.

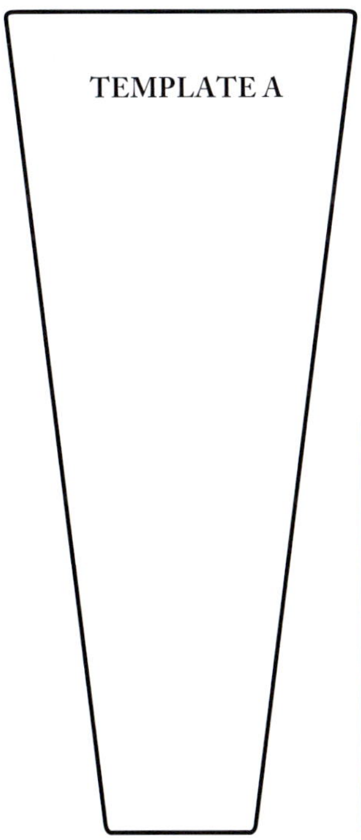

Templates are shown at 70% of actual size. Enlarge on a photocopier.

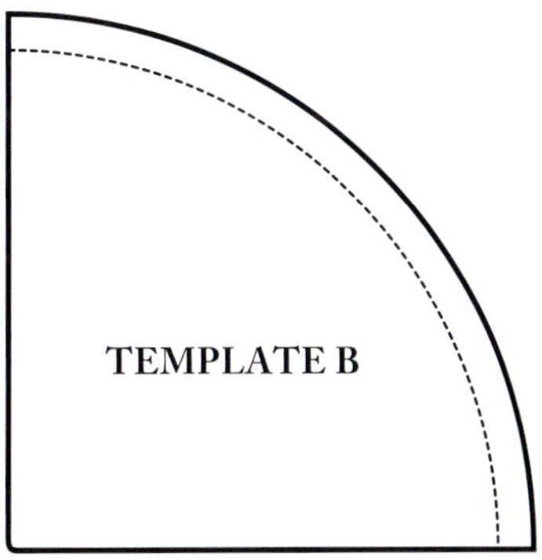

STITCHING

1 Fold each fan segment in half lengthways with right sides together (diagram **A**), then stitch a ¼ in/0.75 cm seam across the wider end (diagram **B**). Clip the corner and unfold. You will now have a piece with a little 'hood' on it (diagram **C**). Make six for each complete fan; there are 36 fans in all.

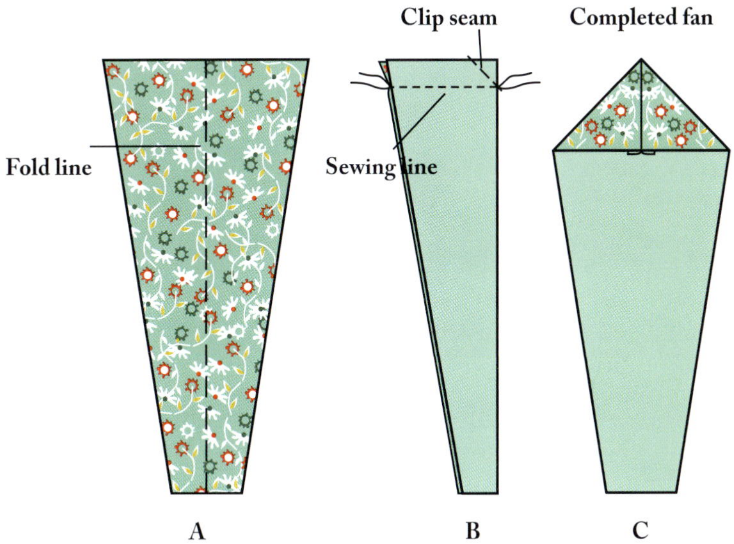

2 Choosing randomly from your fabric selection stitch 6 fan shapes together, press the seams open, remembering to press each seam as you go. Repeat until you have 36 fans in all (diagram **D**).

D

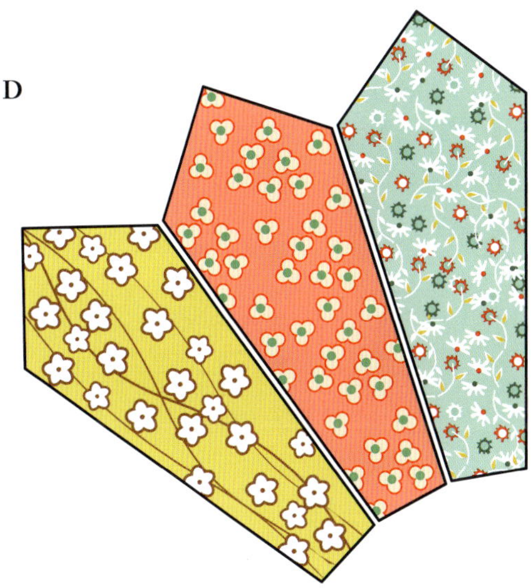

3 To position the fan accurately on the backing square first fold the square in half diagonally and lightly finger press.

4 Place the centre fan seam over the fold and pin in place. You may occasionally need to trim a fraction off at either side. Appliqué in place using a fine hemming stitch and a toning thread.

5 Now turn under ¼ in/0.75 cm on the curved edge of each quarter circle and appliqué over the fan.

6 Using the quilt plan on page 38 as a guide lay out all the blocks and stitch together in rows and then stitch the rows together.

BORDERS

The border is made by stitching the triangles together in rows working from left to right and starting and finishing with a small triangle, matching the ends of the border triangles to the edges of the assembled quilt top.

1 Stitch the corner squares to the top and bottom border strips.

2 Stitch the borders to the quilt sides first and then top and bottom.

FINISHING

1 Measure the quilt top through the centre horizontally and vertically to check your measurements and adjust your wadding and backing fabric to fit.

2 Spread the backing right side down on a flat surface, then, working from the centre outwards, smooth out the wadding and the patchwork top, right side up, on top. Fasten together with safety pins or baste in a grid, working from the centre out.

3 Mark your quilting design on the quilt. Hand or machine quilt the layers.

BINDING

Join the binding strips with diagonal seams to make a continuous length to fit all round the quilt and use to bind the edges with a double-fold binding, mitred at the corners.

TIP This quilt was long-arm quilted but you might like to quilt by hand or machine either echoing the fan shapes or with an overall design of flowers and leaves.

LOOKED AT ANOTHER WAY

This very old and much-loved pattern can be used in many ways and is wonderful for using up scraps. Four blocks make a cushion, 16 make a throw. Be adventurous with your colours and designs.

Folded Pinwheels

DESIGNED BY MARION PATTERSON

This was one of the first quilts I designed and I was inspired by seeing young children with spinning pinwheels at a country fair. It reminds me of happy children and warm summer days and it is also very simple to make. I'm sure it will give you as much pleasure as it gives me.

FINISHED SIZE
29½ x 41½ in/75 x 105.5 cm

YOU WILL NEED
All fabrics are 100% cotton

- **Body of the quilt**
  Fabric 1 – 28 in/70 cm pinwheel background and borders
  Fabric 2 – 24 in/60 cm pinwheel and inner borders
  Fabric 3 – 24 in/60 cm plain squares and borders
- **Backing** 37 x 49 in/ 94 x 124.50 cm
- **Binding** Coordinating colour fabric, 14 in/35 cm
- **Wadding** 37 x 49 in/ 94 x 124.5 cm

CUTTING

Strips are cut across the width of the fabric.

1 **Fabric 1** Cut four 3½ in/9 cm wide strips and then crosscut into 48 x 3½ in/9 cm squares. Cut two 3 in/7.5 cm strips for the borders.

2 **Fabric 2** Cut four 3½ in/9 cm wide strips and then crosscut into 48 x 3½ in/9 cm squares. Cut four 1½ in/4 cm wide strips for the inner borders.

3 **Fabric 3** Cut two 6½ in/16.5 cm wide strips and then crosscut into 12 x 6½ in/16.5 cm squares. Cut two 3 in/7.5 cm strips for the borders.

4 **Binding** Cut four 2½ in/6.5 cm strips.

STITCHING

1 From fabric 2, fold one of the squares diagonally in half with wrong sides together. Fold one point over towards the raw edge corner. Pin the folded triangle to one of the background squares (fabric 1 – diagram **A**). Repeat to make a total of four matching squares, making sure that all the triangles are folded the same way (diagram **B**).

2 Arrange the four squares to form a pinwheel. Stitch the squares together in pairs (diagram **C**) then pin and stitch the two pairs together to form a pinwheel block (diagram **D**). Press the seams open to reduce bulk. Continue until you have pieced 12 pinwheel blocks.

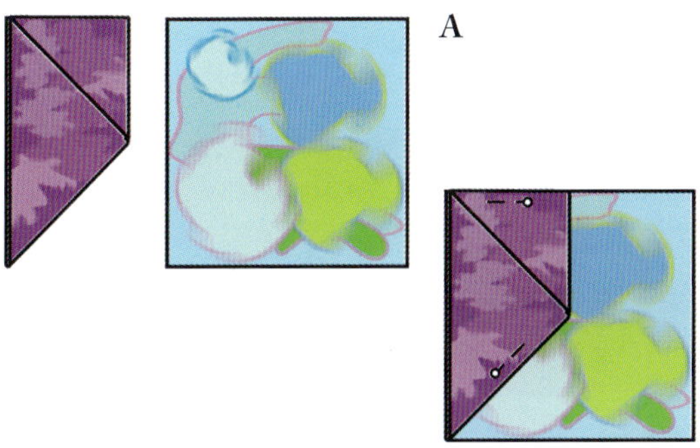
A

B
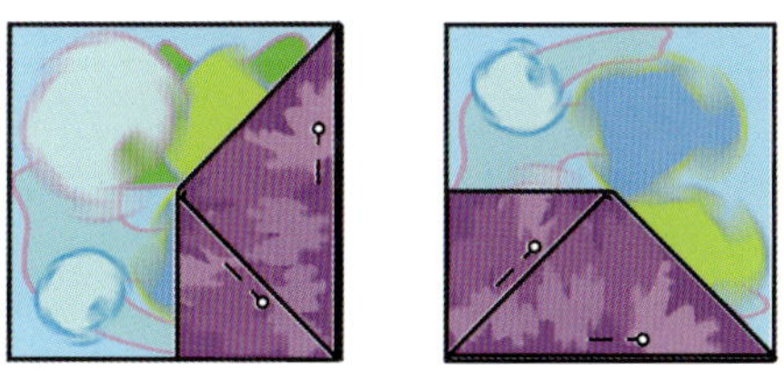

C
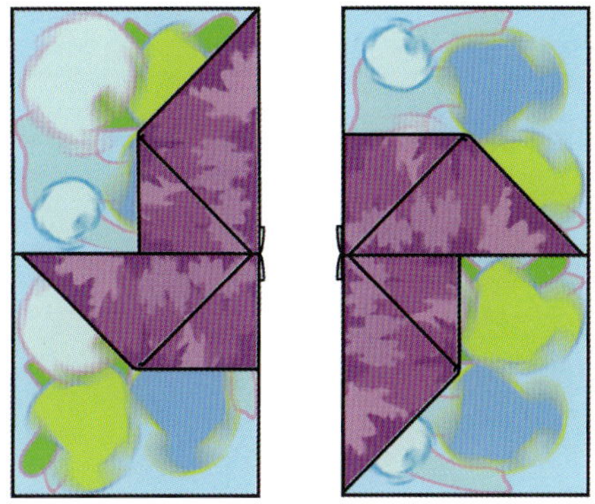

D
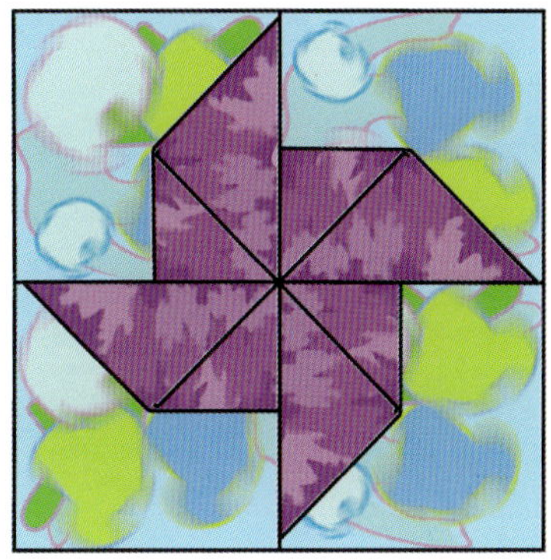

3 Next, pin then stitch the pinwheel block with the plain squares (fabric 3) in rows as follows:
Row 1: pinwheel square, plain square, pinwheel square and plain square.
Row 2: plain square, pinwheel square, plain square and pinwheel square.
Row 3: As row 1.
Row 4: As row 2.
Row 5: As row 1.
Row 6: As row 2.

4 Pin then stitch the rows together making sure that you match the seams.

QUILT PLAN

BORDERS

1 Take your 1½ in/4 cm wide narrow strips of fabric 2 and press them in half to give you a ¾ in/2 cm strip. Measure the quilt top through the centre horizontally then cut the strips for the top and bottom of the quilt to the correct length.
2 Pin then stitch one strip to the top edge of the quilt so that the folded side is away from the edge between the top and the border before stitching the latter (you can either pin or machine-baste these in place first). Repeat for the bottom edge.
3 Take one of the border strips from fabric 1 and one from fabric 3 and cut to the same length as the narrow border strip. Pin one of these to the quilt top and one to the bottom then stitch in place. Press the seams to one side.
4 You now need to add the narrow border strips to the sides of the quilt. You will note from the quilt plan on page 44 that the narrow border is not placed along the entire length of the border strip but ends when it meets the narrow border strip already stitched along the top and bottom.
5 Measure the quilt top through the centre vertically to determine the exact length of your remaining narrow border strips then add 1 in/2.5 cm on to this measurement. Cut your two remaining 1½ in/4 cm wide narrow strips of fabric (fabric 2) and turn under ½ in/1.25 cm at each end then press it in half as for other narrow borders to give you a ¾ in/2 cm strip. Pin on the quilt on each side making sure that the ends are level with the narrow border at the top and bottom of the quilt then stitch in place.
6 Re-measure the quilt, this time taking an exact length measurement. Take your two remaining border strips from fabrics 1 and 3 and cut to size. Pin these to the sides of the quilt and stitch in place. Press the seams to one side.

FINISHING

1 Mark your quilting design on the quilt.
2 Spread the backing right side down on a flat surface. Working from the centre out, smooth out the wadding and the patchwork top, right side up, on top. Fasten together with safety pins or baste in a grid.
3 Hand or machine quilt the layers.
4 Stitch the binding strips with diagonal seams to make a continuous length to fit all round the quilt and use to bind the edges with a double-fold binding, mitred at the corners.

LOOKED AT ANOTHER WAY

Why not make the quilt using one background fabric and four different coloured fabrics for the pinwheel? Whether the pinwheel is multi-colour or not, it makes a wonderful focal point for cushion covers and other accessories.

Christmas Table Runner

DESIGNED BY SALLY ABLETT

This quick-to-make table runner would grace any table at any time of the year. Why not make one for each season using pastels and brights for spring and summer or beautiful subdued tones for autumn?

FINISHED SIZE
21 x 43½ in/53.5 x 110.5 cm

YOU WILL NEED
All fabrics are 100% cotton

- **Body of quilt**
  Cream fabric: ½ yd/50 cm
  Red fabric: 14 in/35 cm
  Green fabric (for blocks and binding): ⅔ yd/62.5 cm
  Black/green fabric: one fat quarter
  Black/gold fabric: one fat quarter
- **Backing** 24 x 48 in/ 60 x 122 cm
- **Wadding** 24 x 48 in/ 60 x 122 cm

QUILT PLAN

CUTTING

Cream fabric

Cut ten squares 4½ in/11.5 cm.

Cut four squares 5¼ in/13.5 cm, then cut each in half diagonally twice to make 16 triangles in all.

Red fabric

Cut three squares 4½ in/11.5 cm for centre of block.

Cut two strips 2½ x 17½ in/6.5 x 44.5 cm for border.

Cut two strips 2½ x 40⅛ in/6.5 x 102 cm for border.

Green fabric

Cut four squares 5¼ in/13.5 cm, then cut each in half diagonally twice to make 16 triangles in all.

Cut two squares 4⅞ in/12.5 cm, then cut each in half diagonally once to make 4 triangles in all.

Cut four squares 4⅞ in/12.5 cm, then cut each in half diagonally once to make 8 triangles in all.

Cut four squares 2½ in/6.5 cm for border corners

Cut four strips 2½ in/6.5 cm wide for binding.

Black/green fabric

Cut six squares 5¼ in/13.5 cm, then cut each in half diagonally twice to make 24 triangles in all.

Black/gold fabric

Cut one square 5¼ in/13.5 cm, then cut this in half diagonally twice to make 4 triangles in all.

Cut eight squares 4⅞ in/12.5 cm, then cut each in half diagonally once to make 16 triangles in all.

STITCHING

1 Lay out all the pieces as indicated in the quilt plan.

2 Referring to the diagrams on page 50 make up four of diagram A, 12 of diagram B and four of diagram C. Remember to press each seam as you stitch to achieve the best result.

3 Using the quilt plan as a guide lay out the blocks and stitch them together in diagonal rows beginning at the top left corner of the quilt. Stitch the rows together.

A

B

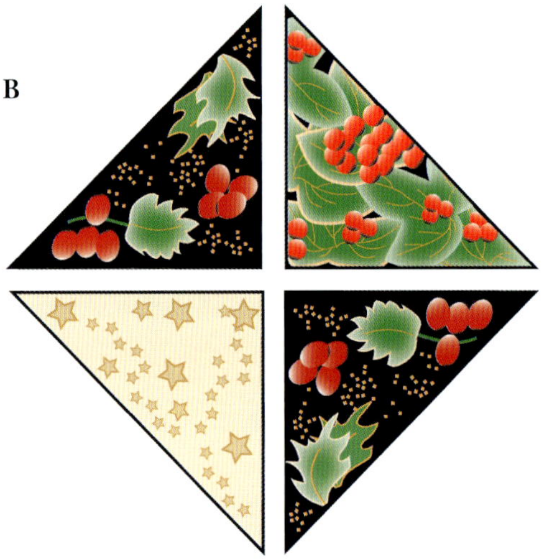

C

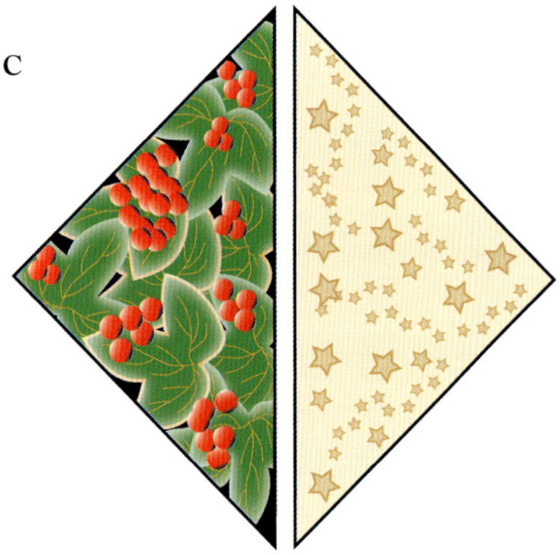

BORDERS

Stitch the corner squares to the top and bottom strips. Attach the side strips first and then the top and bottom strips.

FINISHING

1 Measure the quilt top through the centre horizontally and vertically to check your measurements and adjust your wadding and backing fabric to fit.
2 Spread the backing right side down on a flat surface, then, working from the centre outwards, smooth out the wadding and the patchwork top, right side up, on top. Fasten together with safety pins or baste in a grid, working from the centre out.
3 Mark your quilting design on the quilt. Hand or machine quilt in the ditch using a gold metallic thread to add some sparkle.

BINDING

Join the binding strips with diagonal seams to make a continuous length to fit all round the quilt and use to bind the edges with a double-fold binding, mitred at the corners.

TIP Triangles can be tricky! If they have distorted or stretched, re-size before stitching the blocks together. This will give you perfect squares.

*Metallic thread snaps easily in a machine.
To help prevent this, use a large eyed needle and to ease the tension use an overlocker thread holder placed a short distance from your machine.

LOOKED AT ANOTHER WAY

This block adapts easily. Try changing the colour sequence within the block to achieve a different look. Why not make some coordinating table mats to complement to table runner or to be used alone?

Spring Fever

DESIGNED BY MARION PATTERSON

I have made quite a few different pinwheel quilts but had not made one that was pieced on the diagonal with side setting triangles so I thought that it was time I rectified that. I had just received a new delivery of Moda Jelly Rolls and I decided to use them to make the quilt.

FINISHED SIZE
33 x 44 in/84 x 111 cm

YOU WILL NEED
All fabrics are 100% cotton

- **Body of quilt** 1 Jelly Roll (alternatively choose 24 different fabrics approximately one fat eighth in size)

  Coordinating fabric for side triangles and inner borders, ½ yd/50 cm
- **Backing** 41 x 52 in/ 104 cm x 133 cm
- **Binding** Coordinating colour fabric, ½ yd/50 cm
- **Wadding** 41 x 52 in/ 104 x 133 cm

QUILT PLAN

CUTTING

1 Select 24 strips from your jelly roll (or from your 24 selected fabrics) and cut four rectangles 2½ x 4½ in/ 6.5 x 11.5 cm from each and number them 1 to 24.
2 From the remaining fabric cut 60 rectangles 2½ x 4½ in/6.5 x 11.5 cm.
3 From your coordinating fabric cut two 2½ in/6.5 cm strips across the width of the fabric and cross-cut into 20 x 2½ in/6.5 cm squares.
4 Cut four strips 1½ in/4 cm across the width of the fabric for the narrow border.
5 Cut four squares 4½ in/11.5 cm for the border corners.
6 Cut five strips 2½ in/6.5 cm for the binding.

STITCHING

1 Using diagram A and the piecing instructions that follow, stitch the squares and rectangles into blocks using a ¼ in/0.75 cm seam allowance.

2 Pin then stitch the blocks together in diagonal rows until all ten rows have been completed (diagram **B**). Then pin and stitch the rows together.

A

NOTE You will find it easier to work on one complete row at a time. When each row is finished, label it with the row number so that you don't get them mixed up.

B

PIECING INSTRUCTIONS

Row 1	Fabric 1 plus square
	Fabric 1 plus square
Row 2	Fabric 3 plus square
	Fabric 3 and Fabric 1
	Fabric 1 and Fabric 2
	Fabric 2 plus square
Row 3	Fabric 4 plus square
	Fabric 4 and Fabric 3
	Fabric 3 and Fabric 5
	Fabric 5 and Fabric 2
	Fabric 2 and Fabric 6
	Fabric 6 plus square
Row 4	Fabric 7 plus square
	Fabric 7 and Fabric 4
	Fabric 4 and Fabric 8
	Fabric 8 and Fabric 5
	Fabric 5 and Fabric 9
	Fabric 9 and Fabric 6
	Fabric 6 and Fabric 10
	Fabric 10 plus square
Row 5	Fabric 11 plus square
	Fabric 11 and Fabric 7
	Fabric 7 and Fabric 12
	Fabric 12 and Fabric 8
	Fabric 8 and Fabric 13
	Fabric 13 and Fabric 9
	Fabric 9 and Fabric 14
	Fabric 14 and Fabric 10
	Fabric 10 plus square
Row 6	Fabric 15 plus square
	Fabric 15 and Fabric 11
	Fabric 11 and Fabric 16
	Fabric 16 and Fabric 12
	Fabric 12 and Fabric 17
	Fabric 17 and Fabric 13
	Fabric 13 and Fabric 18
	Fabric 18 and Fabric 14
	Fabric 14 plus square
Row 7	Fabric 15 plus square
	Fabric 15 and Fabric 19
	Fabric 19 and Fabric 16
	Fabric 16 and Fabric 20
	Fabric 20 and Fabric 17
	Fabric 17 and Fabric 21
	Fabric 21 and Fabric 18
	Fabric 18 plus square
Row 8	Fabric 19 plus square
	Fabric 19 and Fabric 22
	Fabric 22 and Fabric 20
	Fabric 20 and Fabric 23
	Fabric 23 and Fabric 21
	Fabric 21 plus square
Row 9	Fabric 22 plus square
	Fabric 22 and Fabric 24
	Fabric 24 and Fabric 23
	Fabric 23 plus square
Row 10	Fabric 24 plus square
	Fabric 24 plus square

3 Trim the edges evenly on all four sides ¼ in/0.75 cm outside the seams so that the quilt centre measures approx 23¼ x 34 in/58.75 x 87.5 cm to the raw edge (diagram **C**).

C

BORDERS

1 Measure the quilt top through the centre vertically to determine the exact length of your border strips. Cut two of your 1½ in/4 cm wide strips for your narrow borders to the appropriate length and stitch to the sides of the quilt top.

2 Measure the quilt top again this time through the centre horizontally then cut the remaining two strips to the correct width and stitch to the top and bottom of the quilt.

3 The outer border is made from the strips you have left over after cutting the rectangles. You will need approximately 60 rectangles 2½ x 4½ in/6.5 x 11.5 cm (12 for the top and bottom and 18 for each side). Stitch together the longest sides of the 4½ in/11.5 cm rectangles in two sets of 12 and two sets of 18.

4 Measure your quilt top through the centre vertically as before then take the two longest assembled border strips (making sure that they are the correct length) and pin then stitch to the sides of the quilt.

5 Re-measure the quilt top again, this time through the centre horizontally up to the outside edge of the inner border and add ½ in/1.25 cm. Cut the assembled borders to fit and add a corner blocks to each end of the borders. Pin then stitch to top and bottom of the quilt.

FINISHING

1 Mark your quilting design on the quilt.

2 Spread the backing right side down on a flat surface, then, working from the centre out, smooth out the wadding and the patchwork top, right side up, on top. Fasten together with safety pins or baste in a grid.

3 Hand or machine quilt the layers.

BINDING

Stitch the binding strips with diagonal seams to make a continuous length to fit all round the quilt and use to bind the edges with a double-fold binding, mitred at the corners.

LOOKED AT ANOTHER WAY

The quilt can be made from your stash of scrap fabrics and plain borders. If you have lots of fabrics in varying shades and patterns of say one colour, they could be used instead of a Jelly Roll.

Pathways

DESIGNED BY SALLY ABLETT

This pretty quilt would brighten any bedroom and is very straightforward to make. It can be made to suit either a boy or a girl and would make an ideal teenager's quilt. It is as versatile as your imagination.

FINISHED SIZE
46½ x 60½ in/118 x 153.75 cm

YOU WILL NEED
All fabrics are 100% cotton

- **Body of Quilt**
  Background fabric:
  2½ yds/2.3 mtrs
- Pink fabric:
  ⅜ yd/34 cm
- Dark purple fabric:
  ⅜ yd/34 cm
- Light purple fabric:
  ⅜ yd/34 cm
- Yellow fabric: ⅜ yd/34 cm
- Blue fabric: ⅜ yd/34 cm
- Green fabric: ½ yd/50 cm
- Orange fabric: ⅜ yd/34 cm
- **Backing** 54½ x 68½ in/
  138.5 x 174 cm
- **Wadding** 54½ x 68½ in/
  138.5 x 174 cm

QUILT PLAN

CUTTING

Background fabric
48 strips 2½ x 8½ in/6.5 x 22 cm.
82 strips 1⅞ x 6⅞ in/4.75 x 17.5 cm
– trim 45° at each side of piece.
14 strips 1⅞ x 3⅝ in/4.75 x 9.25 cm
– trim 45° at right side of piece.
14 strips 1⅞ x 3⅝ in/4.75 x 9.25 cm
– trim 45° at left side of piece.
6 strips 2¼ in/5.5 cm across the width of the fabric for the binding.

Pink fabric
2 strips 2½ x 14⅝ in/6.5 x 37.25 cm for top and bottom of border.
8 squares 4⅞ in/12.5 cm cut in half diagonally once.
8 squares 2⅞ in/7.25 cm cut in half diagonally once.
4 squares 2½ in/6.5 cm.

Dark purple fabric
2 strips 2½ x 14⅝ in/6.5 x 37.25 cm for sides of border.
4 squares 4⅞ in/12.5 cm cut in half diagonally once.
4 squares 3¾ in/9.5 cm cut in half diagonally once.
1 square 4 in/10.25 cm cut in half diagonally twice.
4 squares 2⅞ in/7.25 cm cut in half diagonally once.
2 squares 3¼ in/8 cm cut in half diagonally twice.
1 square 2½ in/6.5 cm.

Light purple fabric
2 strips 2½ x 14⅝ in/6.5 x 37.25 cm for sides of border.
8 squares 4⅞ in/12.5 cm cut in half diagonally once.
8 squares 2⅞ in/7.25 cm cut in half diagonally once.
4 squares 2½ in/6.5 cm.

Yellow fabric
2 strips 2½ x 14⅝ in/6.5 x 37.25 cm for top and bottom of border.
8 squares 4⅞ in/12.5 cm cut in half diagonally once.
8 squares 2⅞ in/7.25 cm cut in half diagonally once.
4 squares 2½ in/6.5 cm.

Blue fabric
2 strips 2½ x 14⅝ in/6.5 x 37.25 cm for sides of border.
5 squares 4⅞ in/12.5 cm cut in half diagonally once.
5 squares 2⅞ in/7.25 cm cut in half diagonally once.
2 squares 3¾ in/9.5 cm cut in half diagonally once.
1 square 4 in/10.25 cm cut in half diagonally twice.
1 square 3¼ in/8 cm cut in half diagonally twice.
2 squares 2½ in/6.5 cm.

Green fabric
8 strips 2½ x 7½ in/6.5 x 19 cm for sides and top and bottom of border.
3 squares 4⅞ in/12.5 cm cut in half diagonally once.
6 squares 3¾ in/9.5 cm cut in half diagonally once.
3 squares 2⅞ in/7.25 cm cut in half diagonally once.
2 squares 4 in/10.25 cm cut in half diagonally twice.
3 squares 3¼ in/8 cm cut in half diagonally twice.

Orange fabric
5 squares 4⅞ in/12.5 cm cut in half diagonally once.
2 squares 3¾ in/9.5 cm cut in half diagonally once.
5 squares 2⅞ in/7.25 cm cut in half diagonally once.
1 square 4 in/10.25 cm cut in half diagonally twice.
1 square 3¼ in/8 cm cut in half diagonally twice.
6 squares 2½ in/6.5 cm (corner posts).

STITCHING

The quilt is made up of four quarter blocks, 10 half blocks and 18 full blocks. Use the quilt plan on page 60 as a guide for colour sequence and block and sashing placement.

1 Diagram A shows the corner block, which is made up in two halves. Lay out all the pieces required and stitch pieces 1, 2 and 3 in sequence, press the seams toward the large triangle and repeat for the other half. Stitch the two halves together and add the sashing strip. Make the other three corners in the same way.

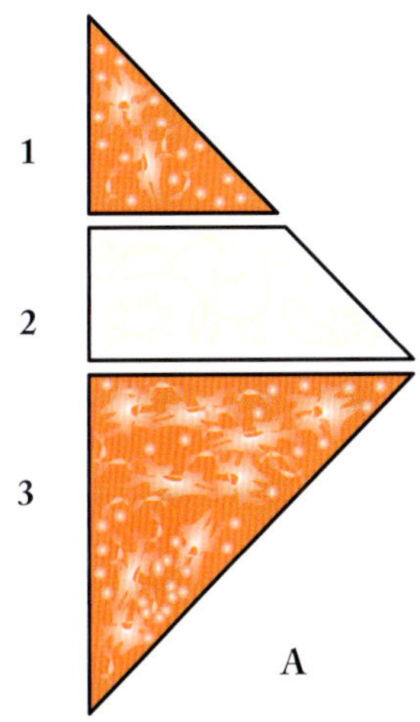

2 Diagram B shows the half block, used around the sides, top and bottom of the quilt and made up of three elements. Lay out all the pieces required and stitch pieces 1, 2 and 3 together in sequence. Press the seams toward the large triangle and repeat for pieces 4, 5 and 6 and pieces 7, 8 and 9. You will now have two triangles and a square. Stitch these together to make a large triangle following the colour sequence. Press seams. Make the other nine half blocks in the same way.

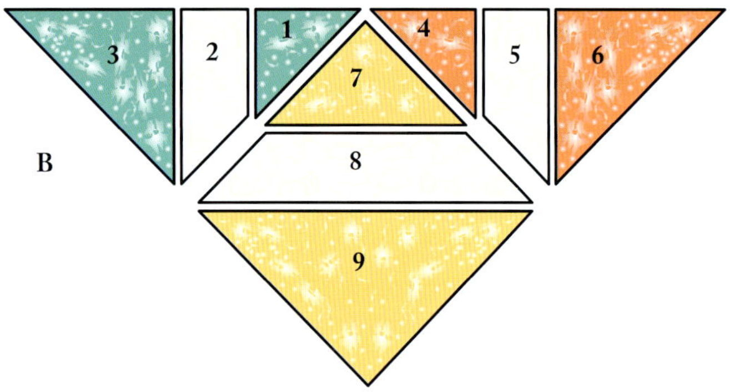

B

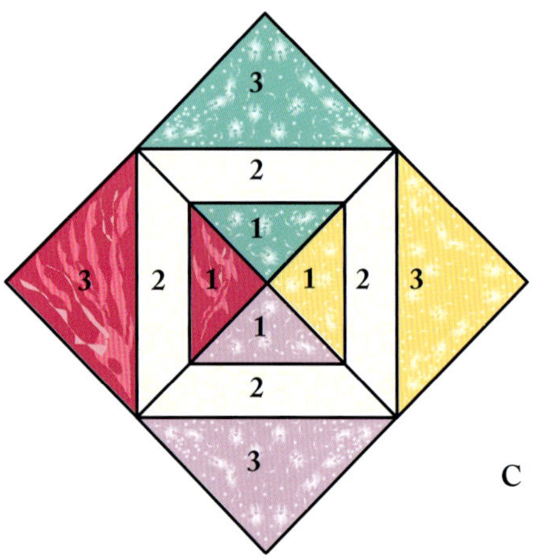

C

3 Diagram C shows the full block, made up of four created squares. Lay out the pieces for each full block using the quilt plan on page 60 as a guide. For each block stitch pieces 1, 2 and 3 together in sequence to make a square, pressing the seams toward the large triangle. Repeat three times. Stitch the four squares together to complete the block. Stitch a background fabric strip to the top and bottom of each block. Repeat until all 18 blocks are complete.

SASHING

The quilt is stitched together in diagonal rows working from the top left hand corner.

1 Using the quilt plan on page 60 as a guide, make up the corner piece adding the small triangles and background sashing strip.

2 Stitch each row in the same way, then when all the rows have been made stitch them together from top left corner to bottom right corner.

BORDER

1 Using the quilt plan on page 60 as a guide for colour placement, join the border strips together.

2 Pin, then stitch the side borders to the quilt

3 Add the corner squares to each end of the top and bottom border strips and stitch to the quilt.

FINISHING

1 Measure the quilt top through the centre horizontally and vertically to check your measurements and adjust your wadding and backing fabric to fit.

2 Spread the backing right side down on a flat surface, then, working from the centre outwards, smooth out the wadding and the patchwork top, right side up, on top. Fasten together with safety pins or baste in a grid, working from the centre out.

3 Mark your quilting design on the quilt. Quilt 'in the ditch' either by hand or machine.

BINDING

Join the binding strips with diagonal seams to make a continuous length to fit all round the quilt and use to bind the edges with a double-fold binding, mitred at the corners.

LOOKED AT ANOTHER WAY

Be bold with this one! Raid your fabric stash and try colour mixes you don't normally use. You may surprise yourself and discover some unusual colour combinations that really work.

Fireglow

DESIGNED BY MARION PATTERSON

This is a variation on the 'quilt as you go' technique; it takes a little more effort but I like it because it works very well with really bold colourways. Also, the sharper the contrast in tone of the colours you use, the greater the impression of depth is given to the design. Go on be brave! This design is fully reversible, too, so you can use either side, depending upon your mood.

FINISHED SIZE
36 x 45 in/91.5 x 115 cm

YOU WILL NEED
All fabrics are 100% cotton

- **Body of quilt** Two colour groups are used for the front of the quilt, each graduating from darkest to lightest as follows:
  Fabric 1 (darkest) – ⅝ yd/60 cm of each colour
  Fabric 2 – ½ yd/50 cm of each colour
  Fabric 3 – ⅜ yd/34 cm of each colour
  Fabric 4 – ¼ yd/25 cm of each colour
  Fabric 5 (lightest) – ⅛ yd/15 cm of each colour
- **Backing** Coordinating or different colourway fabric, twenty squares 10 in/25.5 cm
- **Sashing/Binding** Coordinating fabric for front of quilt (side A), 30 in/75 cm
  Coordinating fabric for back of quilt (side B), 1 yd/1 mtr
- **Wadding** 20 squares of wadding 9½ in/24 cm
- A walking foot for your sewing machine is essential as you will be 'quilting as you go' through three layers.

NOTE I suggest that you use 100% cotton or 80/20 cotton wadding as it helps make the adhesion of the fabric to the wadding better. Fusible wadding can also be used but I would advise against using polyester wadding, as there is a greater tendency for the fabric to slip when using this 'quilt as you go' technique.

QUILT PLAN

CUTTING

Strips are cut across the width of the fabric.
From each colour group cut the following:

Fabric 1 Cut seven strips 1¾ in/4.5 cm wide.
Cross-cut into 14 in/35 cm strips.
Fabric 2 Cut seven strips 1¾ in/4.5 cm wide.
Cross-cut into 11½ in/29.25 cm strips.
Fabric 3 Cut six strips 1¾ in/4.5 cm wide.
Cross-cut into 9½ in/24 cm strips.
Fabric 4 Cut four strips 1¾ in/4.5 cm wide.
Cross-cut into 6½ in/16.5 cm strips.
Fabric 5 Cut two strips 1¾ in/4.5 cm wide.
Cross-cut into 4 in/10.25 cm strips
Sashing Cut nine strips 1⅛ in/2.75 cm wide from fabric for side A. Cut nine strips 1⅞ in/4.75 cm wide from fabric for side B.
Binding Cut four strips 1⅛ in/2.75 cm wide from fabric for side A. Cut four strips 1¾ in/4.5 cm wide from fabric for side B.

STITCHING

1 Take your 20 10 in/25.5 cm squares and pair them up. Place two squares together right sides facing and draw a line across the diagonal on the wrong side of one square. Stitch ¼ in/0.75 cm either side of this line to give you two half square triangle blocks. Repeat this for all ten pairs (diagram **A**).

2 Cut the triangles apart on the drawn line and press the seams to one side (diagram **B**).

3 Take your squares of wadding and draw a line ¼ in/0.75 cm away from the centre diagonal line. This line will be the placement line for your first strips on side A of the block.

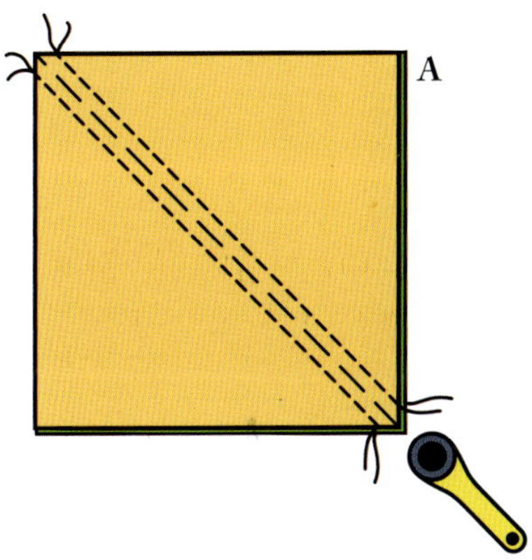

A

B

4 Place the half square triangle block on side B of the 9½ in/24 cm squares of wadding making sure that the diagonal seamline runs in the opposite direction to the line drawn on side A. (You can lightly spray baste or pin in place if desired. However, I find that when using cotton wadding it is sufficient to lightly press.)

5 Turn your block over with the drawn diagonal line uppermost and place your 14 in (35 cm) strips from fabric 1 (with right sides together) on the block against the drawn diagonal line. Pin then stitch on the drawn line using a ¼ in (0.75 cm) seam. Finger press the strips open (diagram **C**).

6 Continue adding the strips to each half of the block (diagram **D**). Do this on all 20 blocks.

C

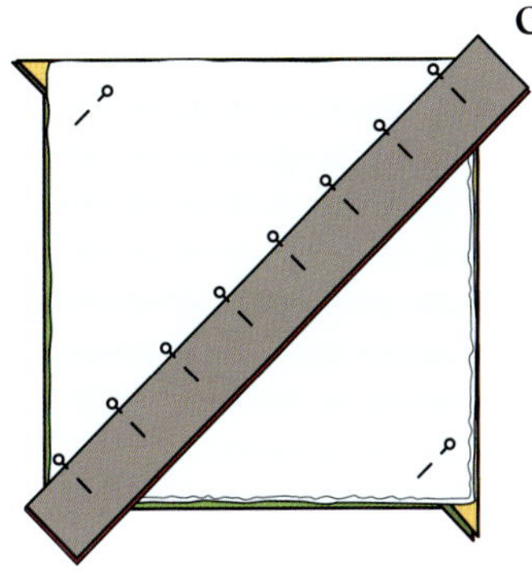

D

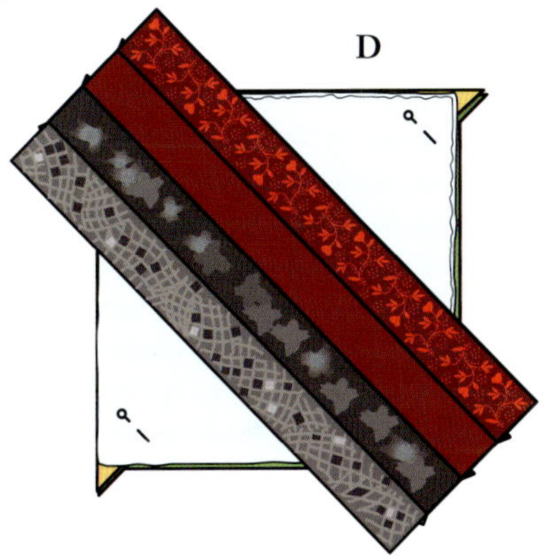

7 You now need to trim down your blocks to 9 in/23 cm using a transparent square. Once all your blocks have been trimmed down arrange the blocks for side A on a design wall or large table. You can use the quilt plan on page 66 as a guide or come up with your own design.

8 Once you are happy with the layout of side A, you need to turn the blocks over to check out the design on side B. Remember that if you make any changes to the layout when looking at side B this will affect the design on side A. Once you are happy with the layout on both sides, add the sashing strips.

9 Fold the 1⅞ in/4.75 cm wide sashing strip in half with wrong sides facing and press. Align the raw edge of the 1⅛ in/2.75 cm wide sashing strip on side A, then place the raw edges of the folded strip on side B (diagram **E**).

E

10 Pin then stitch both sashing strips at the same time to the first block with a ¼ in/0.75 cm seam. Trim the ends of the sashing strips to match the top and bottom edges of the quilt strip. Stitch the second block to the raw edge of the 1⅛ in/2.75 cm wide sashing strip on side A. Continue assembling and joining your sashing strips between the blocks until your row is finished. (diagram **F**).

F

NOTE The edges of the two seam allowances should meet in the middle of the sashing strip. If there is a gap between the two edges, increase your seam allowance. If, however, the two edges overlap, decrease your seam allowance.

11 Pin the folded edge of each sashing strip (side B) in place to cover the seam allowance and slip stitch in place by hand. (You can also stitch this in place by machine.)

12 To join the rows together follow the same directions as for stitching the blocks but use longer sashing strips. If you need to piece your sashing strips, join them first with a diagonal seam. Make sure that you align the vertical strips between the blocks when stitching one row to the next.

FINISHING

1 Fold the 1¾ in/4.5 cm wide binding strip (coordinating fabric for side B) in half lengthwise with wrong sides together and press.

2 With the right sides together and with the raw edges matching, pin then stitch the 1⅛ in/2.75 cm wide binding strip and the folded binding strip together with a ¼ in/0.75 cm wide seam allowance. Press the seam open.

3 Stitch the binding to each side of the quilt first. With right sides together and raw edges matching, stitch the single layer of binding to side A of the quilt.

4 Trim the ends of the sashing strips to match the top and bottom edges of the quilt strip. Fold the binding at the seam line and hand (or machine) stitch in place on the reverse (side B).

5 You now need to attach the binding to the top and bottom of the quilt in the same way but leave a ½ in/1.25 cm tail at the beginning and end. Fold over the ½ in/1.25 cm tail then fold the binding as before and stitch in place (making sure that you slip stitch the side seam in place).

LOOKED AT ANOTHER WAY

This design lends itself to being up or down scaled. Use a combination of narrow and wide strips or have narrow strips on one side and wide strips on the other. Make smaller blocks as place mats or turn into table runners.

Quillow

DESIGNED BY SUE WARREN

Ideal to keep in the car or caravan, where it can be used as a cushion and opened out to use as a quilt to picnic on or snuggle under.

FINISHED SIZE
48¼ x 61 in/122.5 x 155 cm

YOU WILL NEED
All fabrics are 100% cotton

- **Body of quilt**
  Star Centre: ⅜ yd/35 cm

  Star Points, First Border and Binding: 1¼ yds/1.15 mtrs

  Star Background: ⅞ yd/80 cm

  Star Framing: ½ yd/50 cm

  Main Fabric and Second Border: 2¼ yds/2.1 mtrs
- **Backing** 56 x 69 in/142.25 x 175.25 cm for quilt plus a 20 in/51 cm square for cushion back
- **Wadding** 56 x 69 in/142.25 x 175.25 cm for quilt plus a 20 in/51 cm square for cushion front

QUILT PLAN

CUTTING

This quilt is made up of 13 blocks – 12 for the main quilt and one for the cushion front. Cut four strips 4½ in/11.5 cm down the length of the main fabric for the borders before cutting other shapes.

Star Background Cut 52 rectangles 2½ x 4½ in/6.5 x 11.5 cm. Cut 52 squares 2½ in/6.5 cm.

Star Points Cut 104 squares 2½ in/6.5 cm.

Star Centre Cut 13 squares 4½ in/11.5 cm.

Star Framing Cut 26 strips 1 x 8½ in/2.5 x 21.5 cm and 26 strips 1 x 9½ in/2.5 x 24 cm.

Main Fabric Cut six squares 9½ in/24 cm.

Cut four squares 7½ in/19 cm, cut on the diagonal once to form corner triangles. Cut three squares 14 in/35 cm, cut on the diagonal twice to form setting triangles.

Binding Cut 6 strips 2½ in/6.50 cm for main quilt and cushion front across the width of the fabric.

STITCHING

Sawtooth Star

52 Flying Geese units will be needed for the 13 Star Points blocks.

1. Draw a diagonal line on the wrong side of each 2½ in/6.5 cm square of Star Point fabric.
2. With right sides together, position a Star Point square on one end of a rectangle of Star Point background fabric. Align the raw edges then pin and stitch on the pencil line.
3. Trim away the excess fabric to ¼ in/0.75 cm beyond the stitched line.
4. Press the Star Point triangle back, seam towards the background fabric.
5. Repeat for the other side. The finished unit should measure 2½ x 4½ in/6.5 x 11.5 cm.
6. Use the 2½ in/6.5 cm squares of background and the squares cut for the star centres to make up 13 (diagram **A**). The finished Star Block should measure 8½ in/22 cm to the raw edge.

A

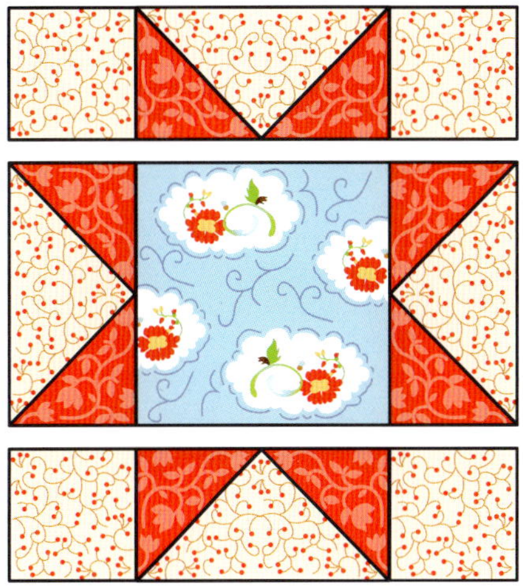

7. Stitch a 1 x 8½ in/2.5 x 22 cm of framing fabric to the top and bottom of each star block.
8. Stitch a 1 x 9½ in/2.5 x 24 cm of framing fabric to either side of the star block. The block should now measure 9½ in/24 cm square.
9. Stitch the blocks together in diagonal rows, adding a setting triangle as shown in the diagram below. To make sure the corners are square find the centre of the corner triangles and match up with the centre of the block (diagram **B**).

B

BORDERS

1 The first border is cut 1½ in/4 cm. Measure the quilt through the width, cut the border fabric to this length, and stitch to the top and bottom edges. Measure the quilt through the length, join the border strips as necessary to make up the length needed, and stitch to either side of the quilt.

2 Measure and stitch the second border as for first border.

FINISHING

1 Measure the quilt top through the centre horizontally and vertically to check your measurements and adjust wadding and backing to fit as necessary.

2 Spread the backing right side down on a flat surface, then, working from the centre outwards, smooth out the wadding and the patchwork top, right side up, on top. Fasten together with safety pins or baste in a grid, working from the centre out.

3 Mark your quilting design on the quilt. Hand or machine quilt the layers.

CUSHION FRONT

1 Stitch corner square triangles to each corner of the remaining star block (diagram **C**).

C

2 Stitch a 3 x 13¼ in/7.5 x 33.75 cm strip of fabric used for the first border to the top and bottom of the cushion front. Add a 3 x 18¼ in/7.5 x 46.5 cm strip of the same fabric to either side.

3 Place the cushion wadding on a work surface with the square of backing fabric right side facing, then the cushion top right side down. Pin and stitch on three sides, leaving the top edge open.

4 Clip the corners and turn through to the right side. Roll the edges between your fingers to give a good edge and tack all around. Quilt the cushion top as desired.

5 Position the cushion front in the centre of one short edge of the quilt, align the raw edges of the quilt and the cushion; the right side of cushion front will be facing the backing fabric. Tack the raw edges of cushion and quilt together.

BINDING

1 Align the raw edges of the binding with the raw edges of the front of the quilt, making sure that the cushion front is sewn through when stitching the binding. Join the binding strips with diagonal seams to make a continuous length to fit all round the quilt and use to bind the edges with a double-fold binding, mitred at the corners.

2 Turn the binding to the back, slip-stitch into place. Slip-stitch two sides of the cushion to the back of the quilt leaving the bottom end open, making sure that the stitches do not come through to the front. A couple of extra stitches will be needed on the two corners for reinforcement.

LOOKED AT ANOTHER WAY

Create lots of different moods – the quilt looks good in strong colours for outdoor use, soft shades for a favourite aunt or fun fabrics for a child or teenager.

Freeform Nine-Patch

DESIGNED BY MARION PATTERSON

I was playing around with some fabrics one day and came up with the idea to make a nine-patch block where the patches were cut "freeform". I hope you enjoy making this quilt as much as I have and remember that there is no wrong way of making it – just a fun way.

FINISHED SIZE
38 x 53 in/96.5 x 134.5 cm

YOU WILL NEED
All fabrics are 100% cotton

- **Body of the quilt** Eight squares of fabric 14 in/35 cm (you need at least four different fabric colourways)

  NOTE Lightly starch the fabric squares as this helps when handling the fabrics.

- **Borders, side and corner triangles** Coordinating colour fabric, 1½ yds/1.4 cm
- **Backing** 46 x 61 in/ 117 x 155 cm
- **Binding** Coordinating colour fabric, ⅜ yd/35 cm
- **Wadding** 46 x 61 in/ 117 x 155 cm

QUILT PLAN

CUTTING

1. Cut eight squares 14 in/35 cm.
2. From your coordinating fabric, cut your border strips first. Cut four strips 4 in/10.25 cm wide lengthways on the straight grain of the fabric. These will be cut to the actual size when the quilt top is assembled.
3. Cut two 16½ in/42.5 cm squares from the same fabric for your side setting triangles. Cut both squares on each of the diagonals to ensure the long side of the triangle will not have a bias edge. This will yield eight triangles but you will only need to use six.
4. You also need to cut two 8⅝ in/22 cm squares for the corner triangles. Cut these in half on the diagonal to yield 4 half square triangles, which will be used on the corners.
5. From the binding fabric, cut five strips 2½ in/6.5 cm wide, across the width of the fabric.

CUTTING/STITCHING

Start by making sure that your 14 in/35.5 cm fabric squares are well pressed and if possible, lightly starched.

Cut 1

1. Layer the squares right side up on your cutting mat. Keeping your squares all together make the first cut approximately one third away from the righthand edge. Make a gentle undulating cut from the bottom of the square to the top.
2. Keeping the squares in order, move the top three on the righthand side to the bottom of their pile. Take the two pieces of each layer and place them right sides together (piece 1 with 2 on top). You will notice that the curves go in opposite directions (diagram **A**).
3. Stitch the pieces together by bringing the edges into position as you stitch, easing them gently as you go. As long as the curves are gentle there is no need to pin. Using a very scant ¼ in/0.75 cm seam, and a slightly smaller stitch length than normal, stitch the smallest secure seam possible. Don't worry if the ends don't match as these will be trimmed later. Work your way down the pile making sure that you keep the stitched squares in order.
4. Press the seam to one side. It may be helpful to use a spray bottle with water to lightly spray the fabric to enable the seams to lie flat.

Cut 2

5. Keeping the squares in the order stitched, turn the squares around 180 degrees so that the stitched seam is now on the left side. Make the second cut as before, approximately one third away from the righthand edge of the square.
6. Move the top piece from the righthand side pile to the bottom. Stitch together as before and press (diagram **B**).

Cut 3

7. Layer the squares on your cutting mat as before (again keeping them in order) then turn all the squares 90 degrees either left or right so that the cut lines are now horizontal. Make the third cut as before on the righthand side.
8. You now need to move the top three layers from the righthand side to the bottom of the pile. Stitch and press as before (diagram **C**).

Cut 4

9. Layer the pressed squares once again then turn the squares 180 degrees and make the fourth cut on the right hand side.
10. Move the top piece to the bottom of the pile. Stitch and press then trim down to 11½ in/29.25 cm (diagram **D**).
11. Attach the side setting triangles to the blocks. Join the diagonal rows together and attach the corner setting triangles (diagram **E**).

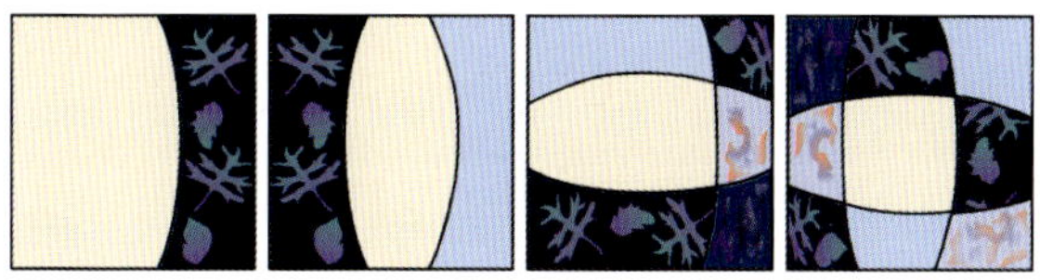

A **B** **C** **D**

BORDERS

1 Measure the pieced top through the centre from top to bottom from the centre outwards to determine the exact length of your border strips. Cut two of your border strips to this length and stitch to the sides. Press the seams towards the borders.

2 Measure the quilt top through the centre from side to side then cut the top and bottom border strips to this measurement and stitch to the top and bottom of the quilt. Press the seams towards the borders.

FINISHING

Mark your quilting design on the quilt top. Spread the backing right side down on a flat surface, then smooth out the wadding and the patchwork top, right side up, on top. Fasten together with safety pins or baste in a grid. Hand or machine quilt the layers.

BINDING

Join all the binding strips into one length and use to bind the quilt with a double-fold binding, mitred at the corners.

E

LOOKED AT ANOTHER WAY

The quilt can be made using bright children's fabrics for a quick and easy child's quilt. You don't always have to have your borders matching. Try making the quilt top with two different colours or even have four different coloured fabrics bordering your quilt.

Quadrants Wallhanging

DESIGNED BY MARION PATTERSON

I originally saw a quilt quite a few years ago with a similar design to this wallhanging. Then a saw a quilt made by Dawn Cameron Dick in the same style and I decided that I just had to make my own pattern, and after quite a few failures I came up with this foundation-pieced version.

FINISHED SIZE

31 in/79 cm square

YOU WILL NEED

All fabrics are 100% cotton

- **Foundation** Calico or Vilene – 28 in/70 cm square
- **Body of quilt** 11 colours ranging from light to dark

  Fabrics 1 to 6: 6 in/15.5 cm each

  Fabrics 7 to 11: 12 in/ 30 cm each
- **Border** Coordinating colour fabric, ½ yd/50 cm
- **Backing** 39 in/99 cm square
- **Binding** Coordinating colour fabric, 14 in/35 cm
- **Wadding** 39 in/99 cm square

CAMELLIA

QUILT PLAN

Arrange your fabrics in the order that they will be used and number them (for example, dark inner triangle graduating to a light outer row). Make sure that you allow extra fabric for seam allowances, i.e. if your drawn strip is ½ in/1.25 cm wide, then cut your strip at least 1¼ in/3.5 cm wide. The excess can be trimmed after adding each row.

DRAWING THE FOUNDATION

1 Cut a square from your chosen foundation (calico or Vilene) about 28 in/70 cm square. (If using calico, spray starch it before drawing your pattern on it as this helps to keep the bias edges more stable when working on it.) Draw two diagonal lines on the foundation piece to give you four triangles.

2 Draw a line 1 in/2.5 cm in from the four sides. (If you want to have a wide outer row, then draw this line 1½ –2 in/ 4 cm–5 cm in from the edge). Label the sides of each triangle A, B and C (diagram **A**). The rows of fabric are only added to sides A and B, not to side C.

A

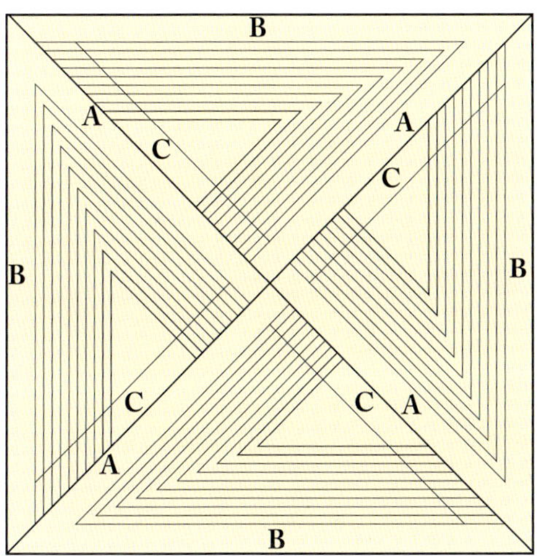

3 You now need to draw your rows on the calico. Using a width of ½ in/1.25 cm, mark your rows (diagram **A**).

4 Once all four triangles have been completed, cut them apart on the original diagonal lines (diagram **B**).

B

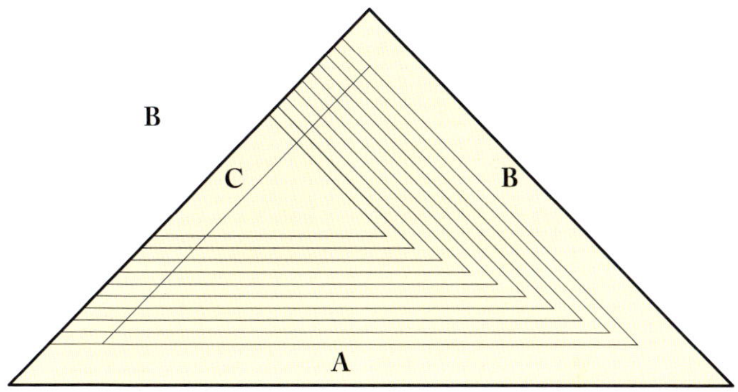

CUTTING

All fabrics are cut across the width of the fabric.

1 **Fabric 1** Cut 4 triangles at least ¼ in/0.75 cm larger than your inner triangle.

2 **Fabrics 2 to 6** Cut 2 strips 1¼ in/3.5 cm wide.

3 **Fabrics 7 to 10** Cut 4 strips 1¼ in/3.5 cm wide.

4 **Fabric 11** Cut 4 strips 2 in/5 cm wide.

5 Cut 4 strips 4 in/10.25 cm wide from border fabric accross the width of the fabric.

6 Cut 4 strips 2½ in/6.5 cm across the width of the fabric for the binding.

NOTE Remember to place your fabrics to be stitched on the side that did not have the lines drawn on. You stitch on the side with the drawn lines.

STITCHING

1 Starting with the centre triangle place it on the foundation and, starting with side A, apply the first row, then side B (diagram **C**).

C

2 Trim back any excess in the seam allowance as you go. Finger press or lightly press with an iron as you go. Keep adding the different strips until the triangle is complete and all the strips for this first triangle have been added. Make up the other three triangles in the same way.

D

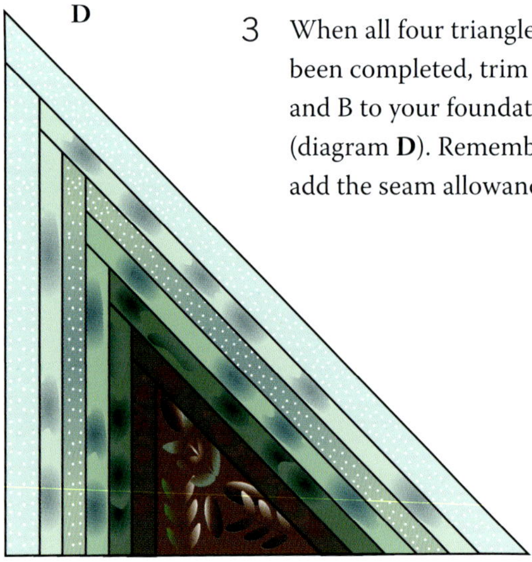

3 When all four triangles have been completed, trim sides A and B to your foundation size (diagram **D**). Remember to add the seam allowance.

4 Stitch two pairs of triangles together then pin and stitch these two pairs together making sure you match the edges. Press the quilt and, if necessary, square off the quilt top at this stage.

BORDERS

1 Measure the quilt top through the centre horizontally and vertically to check your measurements and cut your border strips to fit.

2 Add the borders in the usual way using mitred corners.

FINISHING

1 Measure the quilt top again through the centre horizontally and vertically to check your measurements and adjust your wadding and backing fabric to fit.

2 Spread the backing right side down on a flat surface, then, working from the centre outwards, smooth out the wadding and the patchwork top, right side up, on top. Fasten together with safety pins or baste in a grid, working from the centre out.

3 Hand or machine quilt the layers as desired.

BINDING

1 Join the binding strips with diagonal seams to make a continuous length to fit all round the quilt and use to bind the edges with a double-fold binding, mitred at the corners.

2 Remember to attach a hanging sleeve if required.

TIP I like to use Ultra Fleece or cotton wadding for wall hangings as this tends to help them lie flat.

LOOKED AT ANOTHER WAY

The fabric colours on all the triangles can be reversed to give a different effect (i.e. all light to dark or all dark to light). You could have two triangles with light to dark and two with dark to light.

Square Magic

DESIGNED BY MARION PATTERSON

I was making a quilt using nine-patch blocks and had some left over. I realised that by cutting a nine-patch block and reorganising it I could gain a whole new effect from a very basic pattern. I decided to cut them up and see what design I could create and the result was this quilt.

FINISHED SIZE

46½ in 72 in/118 cm x 183 cm

YOU WILL NEED

All fabrics are 100% cotton

- **Body of Quilt**
  Fabric 1 – 2⅓ yds/2.25 mtrs (dark blue)

  Fabric 2 – 1 yd/1 mtr (light blue)

  Fabric 3 – 1 yd/1 mtr (green)
- **Backing** 54 x 78 in/ 137 x 198 cm
- **Binding** Coordinating colour fabric, ½ yd/50 cm
- **Wadding** 54 x 78 in/ 137 x 198 cm

QUILT PLAN

CUTTING

All strips for the nine-patch blocks are cut across the width of the fabric.

Fabric 1

Cut 10 strips 4¾ in/12 cm wide.
Cut 8 strips 1½ in/4 cm wide for inner border.

Fabric 2

Cut four strips 4¾ in/12 cm wide.
Cut three strips 4 in/10.25 cm for outer border 2.

Fabric 3

Cut four 4¾ in/12 cm wide strips.
Cut three 4 in/10.25 cm wide strips for outer border 2.

BINDING

Cut seven strips 2½ in/6.5 cm.

STITCHING

Make two different strip sets as follows:

SET 1

1 Take one strip from fabric 1 and one strip from fabric 2 and stitch together, then add another strip from fabric 1 to fabric 2 (diagram **A**). Make two of these.

A

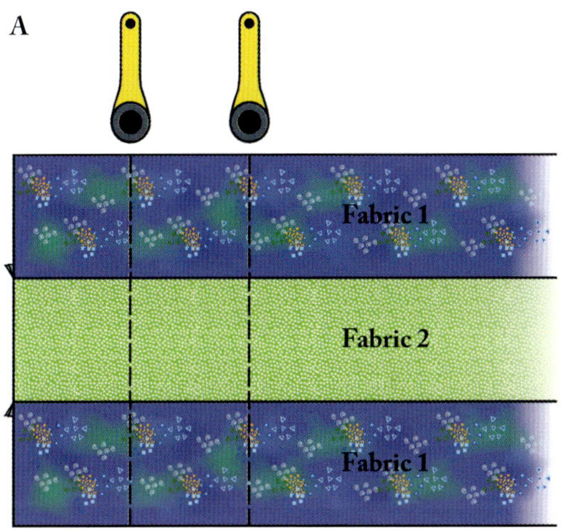

2 Take one strip from fabric 1 and one strip from fabric 3 and stitch together, then add another strip from fabric 1 to fabric 3 (diagram **B**). Make two of these.

B

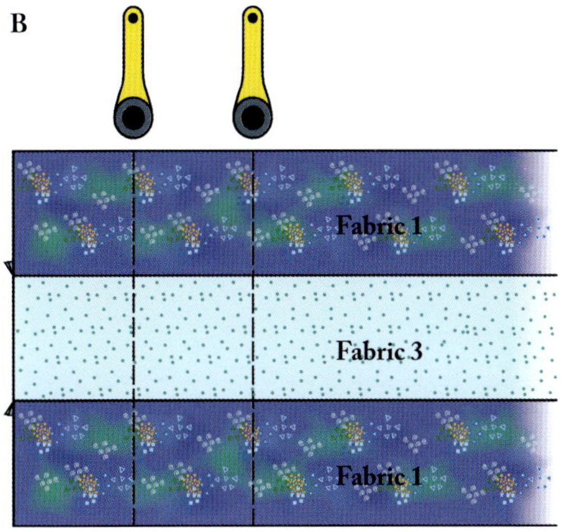

3 Press the seams of set 1 towards fabric 1. Cross-cut these strip sets into 4¾ in/12 cm wide segments. You should get eight from each strip.

SET 2

4 Take one strip from fabric 2 and one strip from fabric 1 and stitch together, then add another strip from fabric 2 (diagram **C**). Make one of these.

C

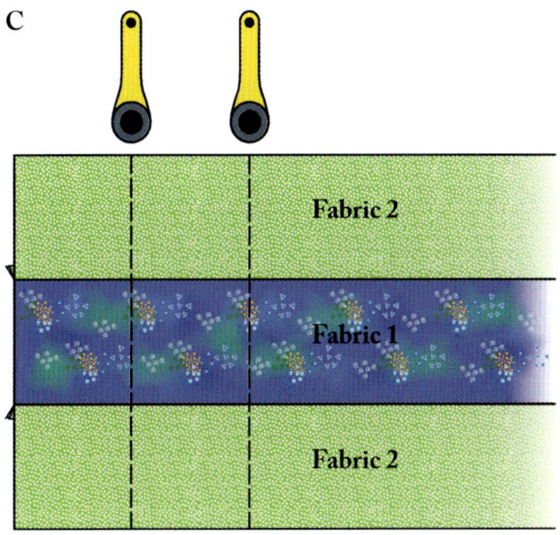

5 Take one strip from fabric 3 and one strip from fabric 1 and stitch together, then add another strip from fabric 3 (diagram **D**). Make one of these.

D

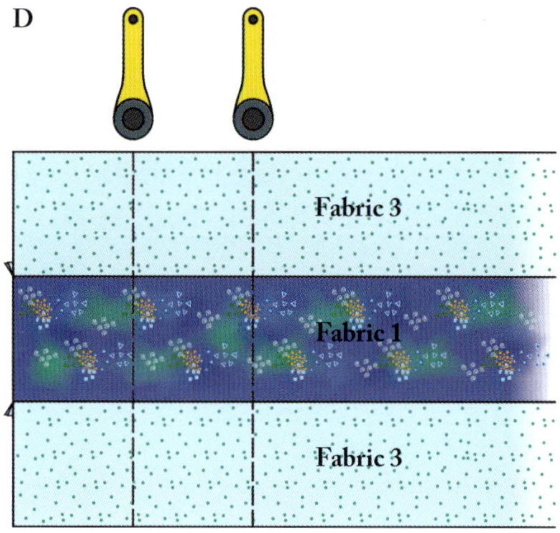

6 Press the seams of set 2 towards fabric 1. Cross-cut these strip sets into 4¾ in/12 cm wide segments. You should get eight from each strip.

7 Make the strips up into 16 nine-patch blocks each measuring approximately 13¼ in/33.75 cm as follows (diagram **E**):

Block 1: Make eight	Block 2: Make eight
Strip set 1(a)	Strip set 1(b)
Strip set 2(a)	Strip set 2(b)
Strip set 1(a)	Strip set 1(b)

E

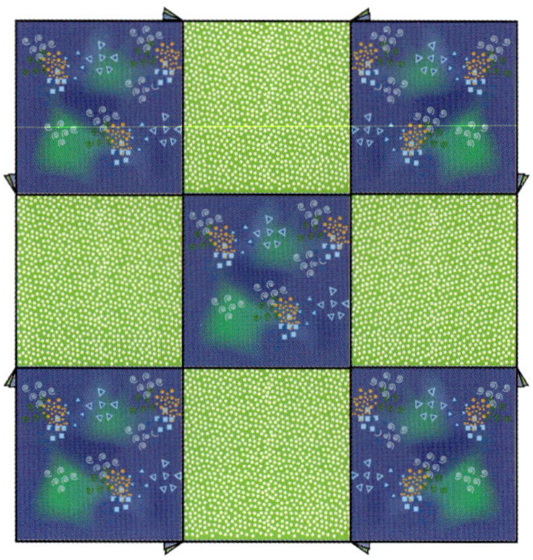

8 Press the seams. Cut the nine-patch into four blocks .

9 Lay out the new blocks using the quilt plan on page 90 as a guide then stitch them into rows. Stitch the rows together pressing the seams as you go.

INNER BORDER STRIP AND BORDER

1 You now need to add the narrow border strips to the sides of the quilt. Measure the quilt top through the centre vertically to determine the exact length. Join the 1½ in/4 cm wide narrow strips of fabric 1 to this length and stitch them to the sides of the quilt. Press the seams to one side.

2 Measure the quilt top through the centre horizontally. Take your remaining 1½ in/4 cm wide narrow strips of fabric (fabric 1) and cut the strips for the top and bottom of the quilt to this width, then stitch them to the top and bottom of the quilt. Press the seams to one side.

3 Once the inner border has been added, you will need to re-measure the quilt both horizontally and vertically and add the outer borders as before.

FINISHING

Measure the quilt top through the centre horizontally and vertically to check your measurements and adjust wadding and backing to fit as necessary. Mark your quilting design on the quilt. Spread the backing right side down on a flat surface, then, working from the centre outwards, smooth out the wadding and the patchwork top, right side up, on top. Fasten together with safety pins or baste in a grid, working from the centre out. Hand or machine quilt the layers.

BINDING

Join the binding strips with diagonal seams to make a continuous length to fit all round the quilt and use to bind the edges with a double-fold binding, mitred at the corners.

LOOKED AT ANOTHER WAY

Instead of using regular cotton fabric try using cotton flannel to make a really warm quilt, perfect for cold wintry nights.

Diamond Quilt

DESIGNED BY SALLY ABLETT

With so many lovely colours in this harlequin of delightful diamonds, this quilt is guaranteed to fit in any room and also to use lots of fat quarters from your stash. The hues can be bright or muted according to your style.

FINISHED SIZE
63½ x 73 in/161.25 x 185.5 cm

YOU WILL NEED
All fabrics are 100% cotton

- **Body of quilt** 30 fat eighths in a selection of different fabrics

  Background fabric 3¼ yds/3 mtrs

- **Backing** 71½ in x 81 in/ 181.5 cm x 205.75 cm

- **Binding** ½ yd/50 cm if made using just one fabric

  NOTE The binding for this quilt was pieced from leftovers. To do the same you need a finished length of 7⅞ yds/7.2 mtrs made of strips 2¼ in/5.5 cm wide.

- **Wadding** 71½ x 81 in/ 181.5 x 205.75 cm

- **Template plastic**

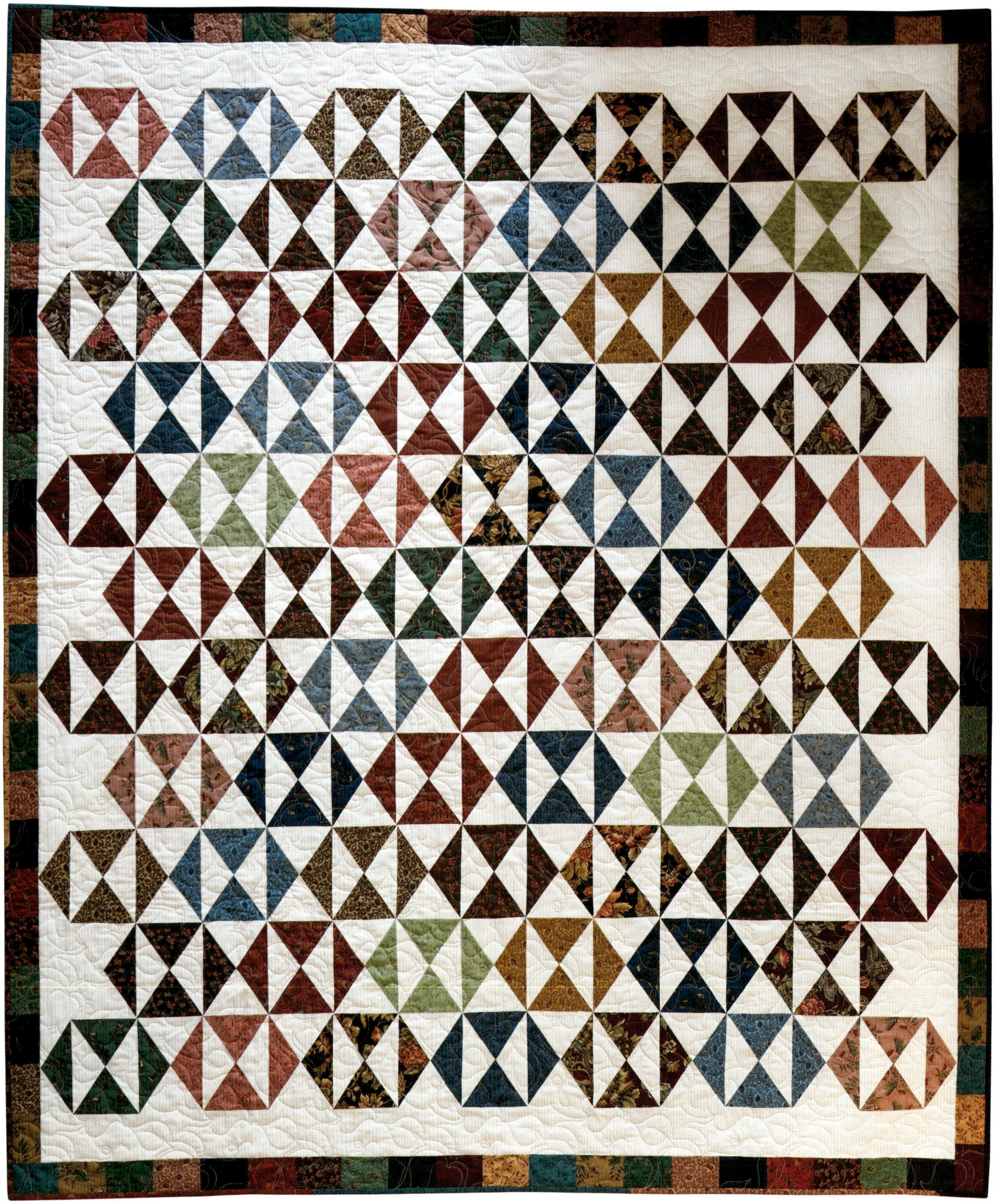

QUILT PLAN

CUTTING

1 Make up all the templates. (* To make template D draw around template E excluding the short side seam allowance, flip the template and complete the drawing.)
2 Cut 144 pieces each from templates A and B using a random selection of coloured fabrics.
3 Cut 144 pieces from template A using background fabric.
4 Cut 144 pieces from template B using background fabric.
5 Cut 12 pieces from template C using background fabric.
6 Cut 10 pieces from template D* using background fabric.
7 Cut 2 left pieces from template E and 2 right pieces from template E.
8 For the border cut enough strips measuring 2½ in x 3½ in/6.5 cm x 9 cm from your coloured fabrics to fit around the quilt's edge.
9 Cut 7 x 2¼ in/5.5 cm strips across width of fabric or piece binding to make required length.

STITCHING

There is only one block used in this quilt so it really is very straightforward.

1 Lay out the colours for each block using the quilt plan on page 96 as a guide.
2 Stitch piece 1 to piece 2 and piece 3 to piece 4. Now stitch the two resulting pieces together to make half the block, press each seam as you go.
3 Next stitch piece 5 to piece 6 and piece 7 to piece 8 and again stitch these two resulting pieces together.
4 Stitch the two halves of the block together and repeat until you have 72 blocks in total (diagram **A**).
5 Once you have all the blocks made lay them out in diagonal rows in order either using the quilt plan on page 96 as a guide or following your own choice and placing the background fabric triangles at each end of the diagonal rows.
6 Starting at the top lefthand corner of the quilt, complete the corner first and work across the quilt stitching in diagonal rows, not forgetting to include the end triangles (diagram **B**).

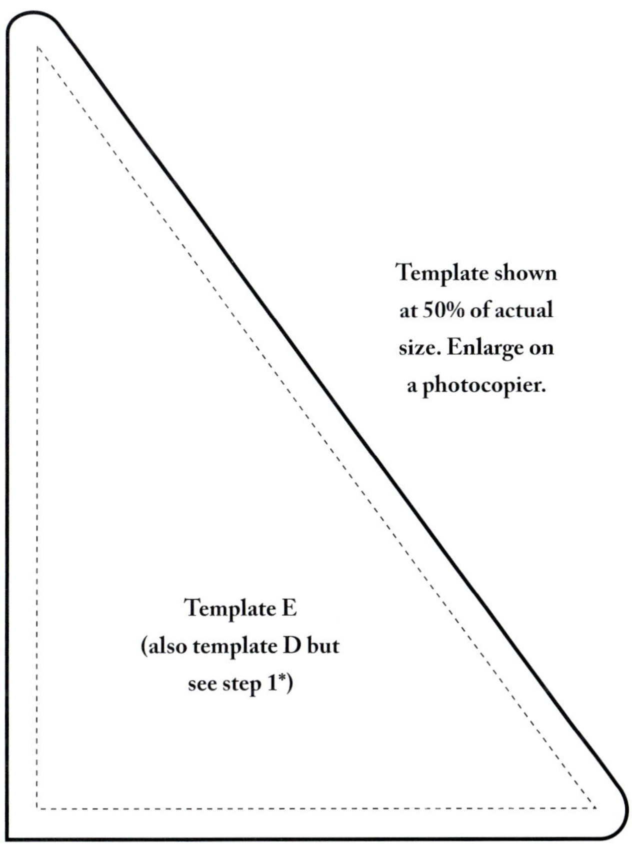

A

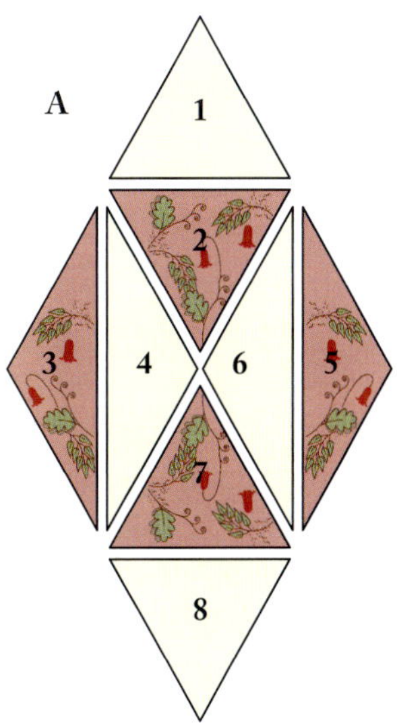

B

BORDERS

1 Measure the pieced top through the centre from top to bottom, then stitch together in strips enough border rectangles to fit each side and the top and bottom edges.
2 Pin, then stitch the side strips to the quilt.
3 Measure the pieced top through the centre from side to side, then pin and stitch the remaining strips to the top and bottom edges.

FINISHING

1 Measure the quilt top through the centre horizontally and vertically to check your measurements and adjust your wadding and backing fabric to fit.
2 Spread the backing right side down on a flat surface, then, working from the centre outwards, smooth out the wadding and the patchwork top, right side up, on top. Fasten together with safety pins or baste in a grid, working from the centre out.
3 Mark your quilting design on the quilt. Hand or machine quilt the layers.

BINDING

Join the binding strips with diagonal seams to make a continuous length to fit all round the quilt and use to bind the edges with a double-fold binding, mitred at the corners.

TIP *Make sure you change your machine needles regularly – this helps to create better stitches and therefore a better quilt.
*If you are using fabrics with different amounts of 'dressing' apply spray starch to the lighter weight fabrics to even the balance.
*A multi-coloured thread would blend very well with this quilt.

Templates A and B shown at 50% of actual size. Enlarge on a photocopier.

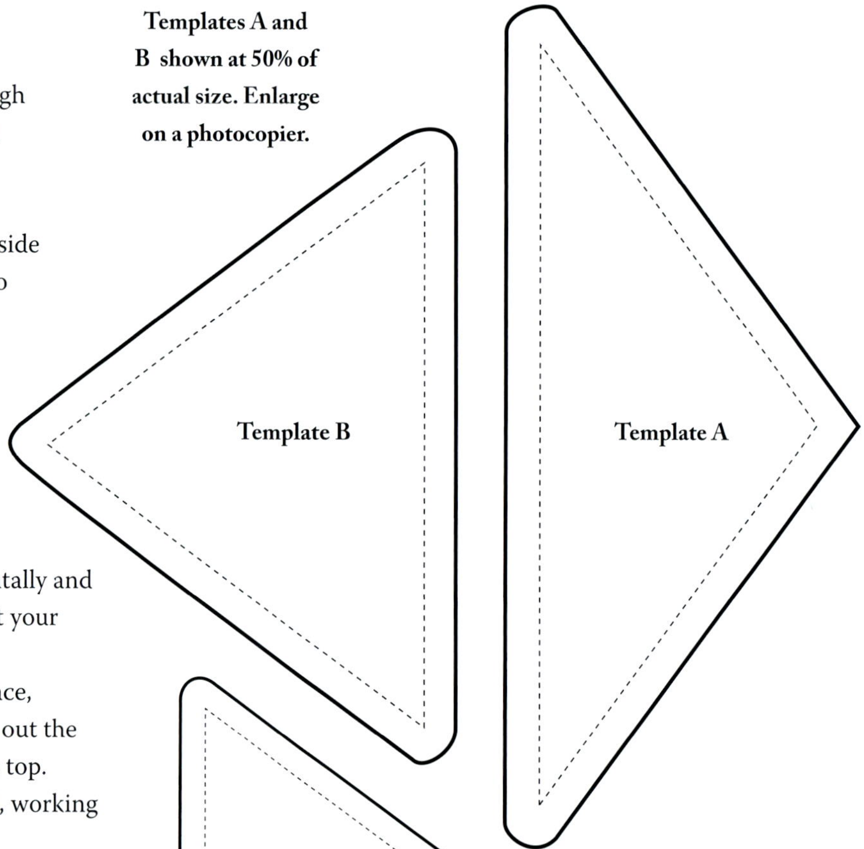

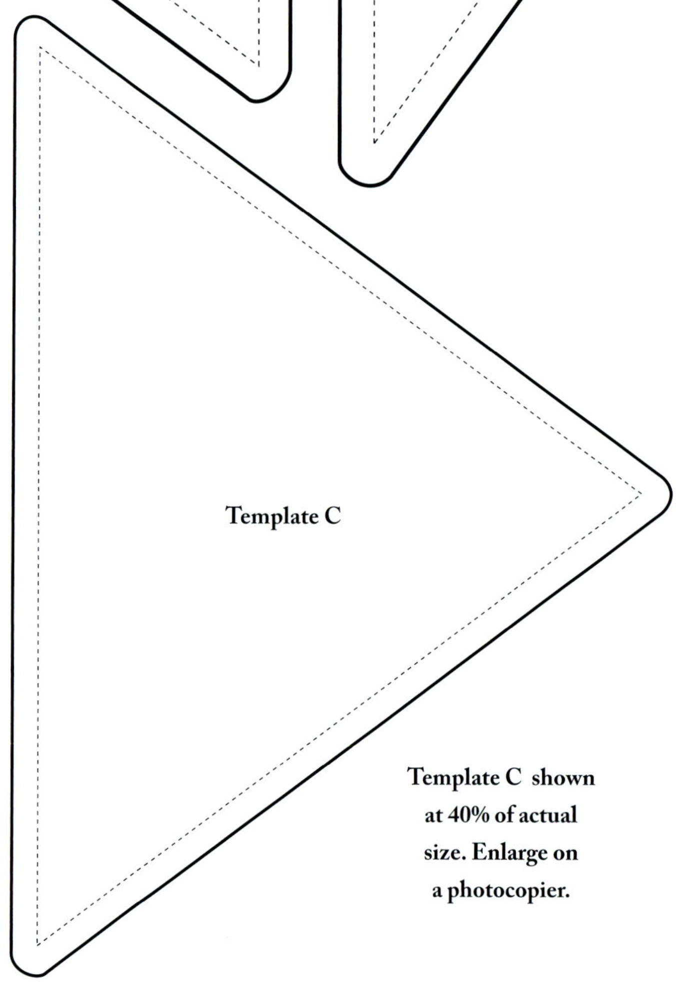

Template C shown at 40% of actual size. Enlarge on a photocopier.

LOOKED AT ANOTHER WAY

Use this straightforward design to practice your colour blending technique, perhaps starting with dark shades in the centre of the quilt fading to light at the edges.

Little Quilt

DESIGNED BY SUE WARREN

This little quilt is a great project to perfect your rotary cutting and/or fast piecing. It could be made for a new baby or as a doll's quilt for a favourite granddaughter.

FINISHED SIZE

28½ x 20½ in/72.5 x 52 cm

YOU WILL NEED

All fabrics are 100% cotton

- **Body of quilt – patch work pattern strips** Light tone fabric, ½ yd/50 cm

  Dark tone fabric, ½ yd/50 cm
- **Backing** 36½ x 28½ in/ 92.75 x 72.50 cm
- **Sashing, borders and binding** Coordinating colour fabric, ⅝ yd/60 cm
- **Wadding** 36½ x 28½ in/ 92.75 x 72.50 cm

CUTTING

Strips are cut across the width of the fabric

1. Cut a strip 2½ x 19 in/6.5 cm x 48.25 cm from each of the light and dark fabrics for the Piano Keys pattern.
2. Cut a strip 2½ x 21 in/6.5 x 53.5 cm from each of the light and dark fabrics for the Chequerboard pattern.
3. Cut one strip 3 in/7.5 cm across the width of the fabric from each of the light and dark fabrics for the Pinwheels; cut eight squares 3 in/7.5 cm from each fabric.
4. Cut two squares 5¼ in/13.3 cm from each of the light and dark fabrics for the Quarter Square Triangles.
5. Cut one strip 2½ in/6.5 cm across the width of the fabric from the dark fabric for the Flying Geese pattern, then cut into eight rectangles 2½ x 4½ in/6.5 x 11.5 cm.
6. Cut one strip 2½ in/6.5 cm across the width of the fabric from the light fabric for the Flying Geese pattern, then cut into 16 squares 2½ in/6.5 cm.
7. Cut two 1½ in/4 cm strips then cross cut to make four 1½ x 16½ in/4 x 42.5 cm strips for the sashing.
8. Cut one strip 2½ in/6.5 cm then cross cut to make two strips 2½ x 16½ in/6.5 x 42 cm for the top and bottom borders.
9. Cut two strips 2½ x 28½ in/6.5 x 72.5 cm for the side borders.
10. Cut three strips 2¼ in/5.5 cm for the binding.

STITCHING

Piano Keys (diagrams **A** and **B**)

1. With right sides together stitch along one long edge.
2. Press the seam allowance to the darker fabric; the strip should measure 4½ in/11.5 cm
3. Cut the strip into four 4½ in/11.5 cm segments.

A

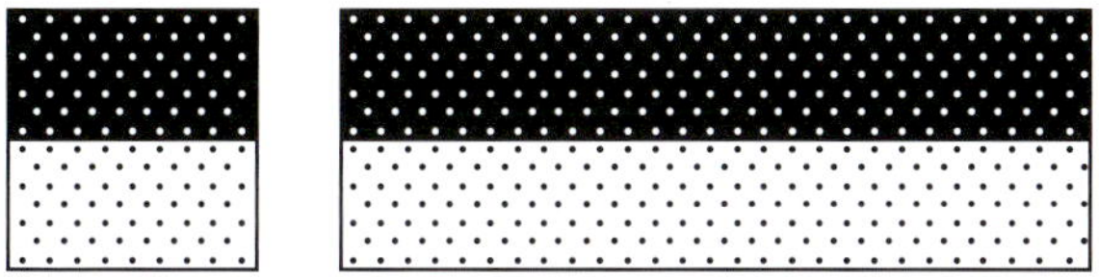

QUILT PLAN

4 Stitch the segments together as shown then press seams to the dark fabric. The finished strip should measure 4½ x 16½ in/11.5 x 42 cm.

B

Checkerboard (diagram **C**)

1 Follow steps 1 and 2 for Piano Keys.
2 Cut the pieced strip into eight 2½ in/6.5 cm segments. The finished strip should measure 4½ x 16½ in/11.5 x 42 cm .

Pinwheels (diagrams **D** and **E**)

C

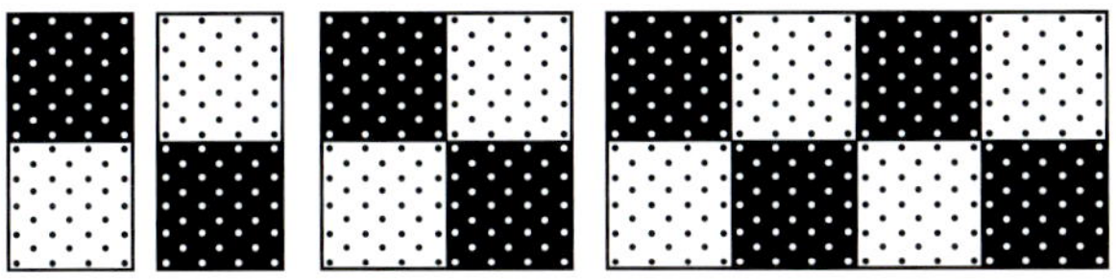

1 Draw a diagonal line on the wrong side of each light square, making sure to go through to the corner points.
2 With right sides together position a light square on a dark square and stitch ¼ in/0.75 cm either side of the pencil line.
3 Cut along the pencil line, open and press seam towards the dark fabric.
4 Trim the square to 2½ in/6.5 cm – trim off two adjacent sides making sure that the seam line meets the right angle of the square.
5 Stitch together four units together to make a pinwheel, the pinwheel unit should measure 4½ in/11.5 cm square. Stitch together four pinwheel units to make the strip. Press the seams open. Finished strip should measure 4½ x 16½ in/11.5 x 42 cm.

D

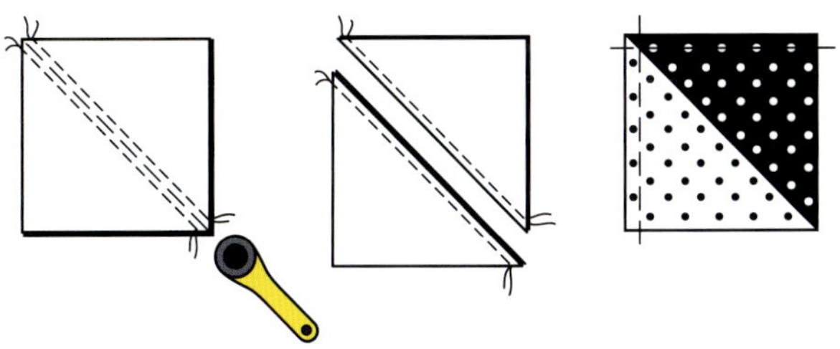

E

Quarter Square Triangles (diagram **F**)

1 Follow steps 1–3 for Pinwheels.
2 Draw a diagonal line on the wrong side of the pieced units (the pencil line will run in the opposite direction to the seam line).
3 Place right sides together with the light triangle on the dark and vice versa. Nestle the seams together, then pin and stitch ¼ in/0.75 cm either side of the pencil line. Cut on pencil line, open and press. The finished unit should measure 4½ in/11.5 cm square.
4 Join four units to make the strip. Finished strip should measure 4½ x 16½ in/11.5 x 42 cm.

F

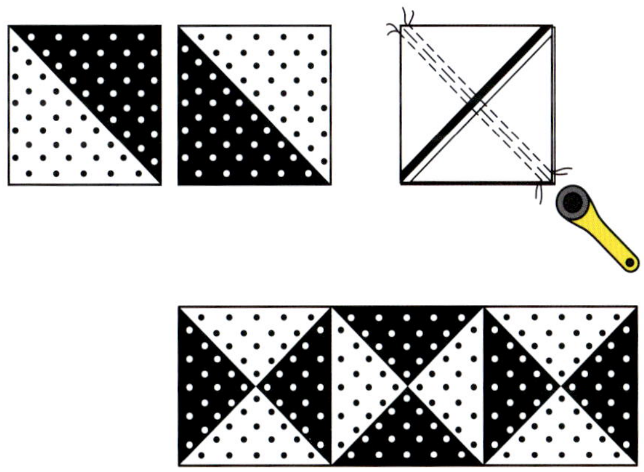

Flying Geese (diagrams **G** and **H**)

1 Draw a diagonal line on the wrong side of each 2½ in/6.5 cm square, making sure to go through the corner points.
2 Place a square on one end of a rectangle of dark fabric, line up the raw edges on three sides and stitch on the pencil line. Trim seam to ¼ in/0.75 cm open out and press toward the light fabric.
3 Repeat for the other side. Each unit should measure 2½ x 4½ in/6.5 x 11.50 cm (diagram **G**).

G

4 Join eight flying geese units together to form the strip. The finished unit should measure 4½ x 16½ in/ 11.5 x 42.5 cm.

H

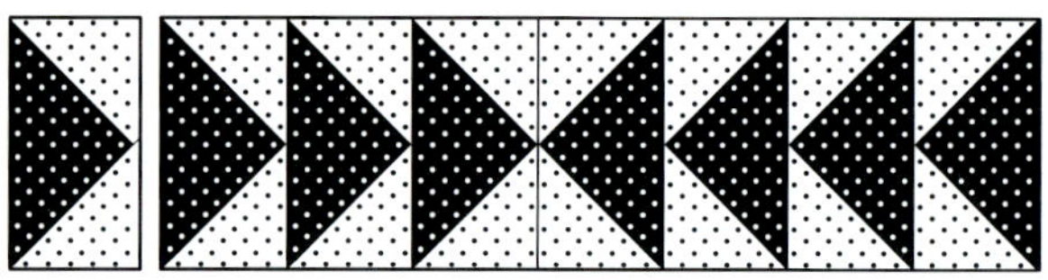

BORDERS

1 Measure the pieced top through the centre from side to side, then stitch two strips of the border fabric to the top and bottom of the quilt.
2 Measure the pieced top through the centre from top to bottom, then stitch two strips of the border fabric to the sides (diagram **I**).

I

FINISHING

1 Mark your quilting design on the quilt.
2 Spread the backing right side down on a flat surface, then, working from the centre out, smooth out the wadding and the patchwork top, right side up, on top. Fasten together with safety pins or baste in a grid.
3 Hand or machine quilt the layers.

BINDING

Stitch the binding strips with diagonal seams to make a continuous length to fit all round the quilt and use to bind the edges with a double-fold binding, mitred at the corners.

LOOKED AT ANOTHER WAY

Have fun playing with colour this quilt will look good in bright or pastel colourways. It also makes a great little wall hanging.

Slap Dash Logs

DESIGNED BY SUE WARREN

These logs are made up of random strips of fabric cut any width between ¾ in/2 cm and 2½ in/6.5 cm. There is no need to be over-accurate in cutting the strips – a slap dash approach will work well. I prefer to use a low-loft wadding for this quilt.

FINISHED SIZE
39 in x 27 in/99 cm x 68.5 cm

YOU WILL NEED
All fabrics are 100% cotton

- **Body of quilt and binding** An assortment of coordinated scraps approximately ¾ yd/70 cm in total
- **Backing** 43 in x 31 in/ 109 cm x 79 cm
- **Sashing and Borders** ¾ yd/70 cm
- **Wadding** 43 in x 31 in/ 109 cm x 79 cm

TIP When making the log blocks it is not necessary to always keep to a ¼ in/0.75 cm seam as long as you stitch in a straight line.

CUTTING

From the Sashing fabric:

Three strips 3½ in x 9½ in/9 cm x 24 cm.

Four strips 3½ in x 21½ in/9 cm x 54.75 cm.

Two strips 3½ in x 39½ in/9 cm x 100.25 cm.

From the fabric used for the logs:

Strips 2½ in/6.5 cm of varying lengths for the binding (you will need 4 yds/3.7 mtrs total length).

STITCHING

1 From one of the log fabrics cut an irregular four-sided shape for the centre (diagram **A**).

2 With right sides together stitch the first log to any side of the centre shape. Let the ends of the log extend beyond the edges of this centre piece.

3 Trim the long ends of the log following the angle of the centre shape.

4 Continue piecing and trimming the logs (diagram **B**). It is not necessary to keep piecing in the usual log cabin sequence; more logs can be added to one or two sides only in order to create an off-centre block if you wish.

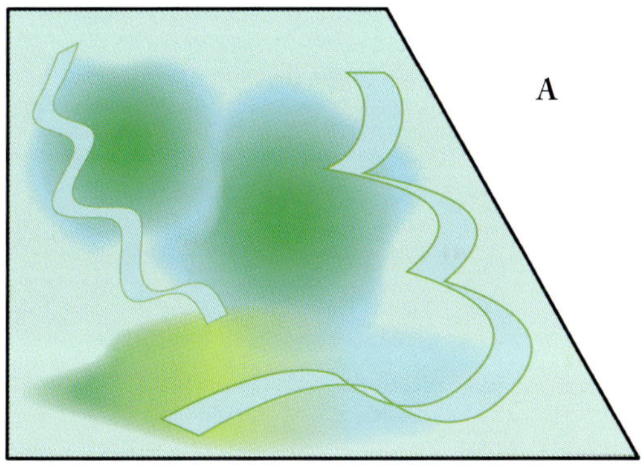

A

B

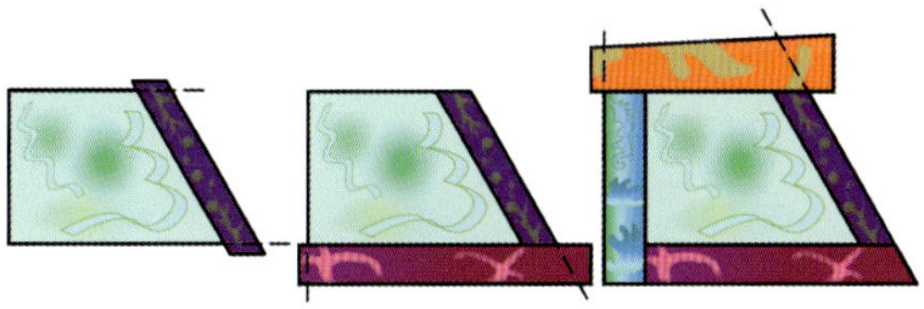

QUILT PLAN

5 Continue adding strips until the pieced unit is more than a 9½ in/24 cm square.

6 Position a 9½ in/24 cm square quilter's ruler on top of the Slap Dash Log and trim off excess fabric to give a 9½ in/24 cm square. If you do not have a ruler, cut a piece of strong card to 9½ in/24 cm and use this to trim the block. Make six blocks (diagram **C**).

C

7 Stitch together three pairs of blocks with a 3½ in x 9½ in/9 cm x 24 cm sashing strip.

8 Stitch a 3½ in x 21½ in/9 cm x 54.75 cm sashing strip between each pair of blocks and to the top and bottom.

9 Stitch a 3½ in x 39½ in/9 cm x 100.25 cm strip to either side (diagram **D**).

D

FINISHING

1 Measure the quilt top through the centre horizontally and vertically to check your measurements and adjust your wadding and backing fabric to fit.

2 Spread the backing right side down on a flat surface, then, working from the centre outwards, smooth out the wadding and the patchwork top, right side up, on top. Fasten together with safety pins or baste in a grid, working from the centre out.

3 Mark your quilting design on the quilt. Hand or machine quilt the layers.

BINDING

Join the binding strips with diagonal seams to make a continuous length to fit all round the quilt and use to bind the edges with a double-fold binding, mitred at the corners.

LOOKED AT ANOTHER WAY

Control the colours of the scraps used to give a pleasing look. The quilt doesn't need to be limited to nine blocks, although this technique is very addictive!

Charmed Table Topper

DESIGNED BY MARION PATTERSON

This quilt came about following the arrival of charm packs. One of my friends wanted a very quick and easy design for a lap quilt for her mother. Using a simple pattern, I was able to put it together in a day and most people could certainly finish it in a weekend.

FINISHED SIZE

35½ in x 41½ in/90.25 cm x 105.5 cm

YOU WILL NEED

All fabrics are 100% cotton

- **Body of quilt** 50 assorted 5 in/12.75 cm fabric squares or one Charm Pack of at least 50 x 5 in/12.75 cm fabrics
- **Side Triangles and Border** Coordinating colour fabric, 22 in/56 cm
- **Backing** 44 in x 50 in/ 112 x 127 cm
- **Binding** Coordinating colour fabric, ⅜ yds/35 cm
- **Wadding** 44 in x 50 in/ 111 x 127 cm

QUILT PLAN

CUTTING

From the border fabric cut the following:

1 Four strips 2 in/5 cm across the width of the fabric for the border.
2 One strip 7⅝ in/19.5 cm across the width of the fabric then crosscut into 7⅝ in/19.5 cm squares. The squares then have to be cut into quarters on the diagonal to give you the side triangles. You will need 18.
3 Two squares 4⅛ in/10.5 cm cut in half on the diagonal for the corner triangles.
4 From the binding fabric, cut five strips, 2¼ in/5.75cm wide, across the width of the fabric.

STITCHING

1 Stitch the squares together in diagonal rows (adding the side setting triangles). Stitch each row in order and label each row to make it easier when joining the rows together (diagram **A**).
2 Once all the rows have been pieced, pin then stitch them together, matching the seams. Press the seams to one side. If the seams in row 1 are pressed to the right then press the seams in row 2 to the left, then row 3 to the right and so on. This will help when matching the seams and reduce bulk.

A

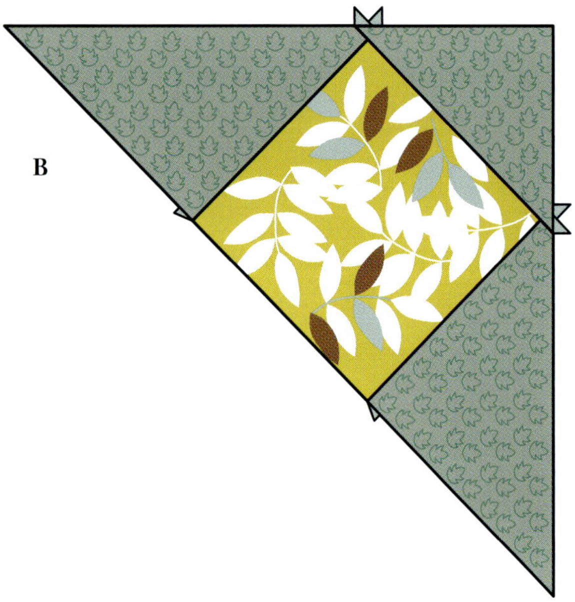

FINISHING

1 Mark your quilting design on the quilt.

2 Spread the backing right side down on a flat surface, then, working from the centre out, smooth out the wadding and the patchwork top, right side up, on top. Fasten together with safety pins or baste in a grid.

3 Hand or machine quilt the layers.

BINDING

Stitch the binding strips with diagonal seams to make a continuous length to fit all round the quilt and use to bind the edges with a double-fold binding, mitred at the corners.

3 Add the corner triangles (diagram **B**).

4 Measure the quilt top through the centre vertically to determine the exact length of your border strips. Cut two of your 2 in/5 cm wide border strips to the appropriate length and add to the sides of the quilt top.

5 Measure the quilt top again this time through the centre horizontally then cut the remaining two strips to the correct width and add to the top and bottom of the quilt.

TIP I suggest that you use 100% cotton or 80/20 cotton wadding as it helps make the adhesion of the fabric to the wadding better. Fusible wadding can also be used but I would advise against using polyester wadding, as there is a greater tendency for the fabric to slip.

LOOKED AT ANOTHER WAY

This pattern is simple but very adaptable, it does not have to be used as a table topper – it could be a lap quilt or wall hanging. You can focus on just a couple of bold colours to highlight a checkerboard pattern or you can mix many fabrics to show off their design. So do just what you fancy, there is no right or wrong way!

Portugal Strippy

DESIGNED BY MARION PATTERSON

One day a customer of mine asked me to help her with a quilt she was making using quarter square triangles. She was having problems with the bias edges stretching and her blocks were coming out in varying sizes. This quilt as you go technique eliminates the problem of bias edges and is quick and easy to do.

FINISHED SIZE
37 x 44¼ in/94 x 112.5 cm

YOU WILL NEED
All fabrics are 100% cotton

- **Body of quilt** Twenty 10 in/25.5 cm squares of fabric (half a Moda Layer Cake pack was used for the front of the quilt)
- **Backing** 1½ yds/1.4 mtr
- **Sashing/Binding** Coordinating colour fabric, 1 yd/1 m
- **Wadding** 1⅓ yds/1.2 mtr
- A walking foot for your sewing machine is essential as you will be 'quilting as you go' through three layers.

QUILT PLAN

CUTTING

1. If you are not using a layer cake cut 20 squares 10 in/25.5 cm from your chosen fabrics.
2. **Backing** Cut four strips from the length of the fabric measuring 10 in x 47 in/25.5 cm x 119.5 cm.
3. **Wadding** Cut your wadding into four strips measuring 10 in x 47 in/25.5 cm x 119.5 cm.
4. **Sashing** From the width of the fabric cut four 1⅛ in/2.75 cm wide strips. Cut four 1⅞ in/ 4.75 cm wide strips.
5. **Binding** From the width of the fabric cut five 2½ in/6.5 cm strips.

STITCHING

1. Take your 20 x 10 in/25.5 cm squares and pair them up.
2. Place the two squares together with right sides facing and draw a line across the diagonal on the wrong side of one square. Pin then stitch ¼ in/0.75 cm either side of this line to give you two half square triangle blocks. Repeat this for all ten pairs.
3. Cut the triangles apart on the drawn line (diagram **A**), open out and press the seams to one side.
4. Put the right sides of two of the half square triangle blocks together with the diagonal seam line matching (make sure that the pressed seams are in opposite directions to reduce bulk) and draw a line on the wrong side of the fabric on the opposite diagonal line. Pin then stitch ¼ in/0.75cm either side of this line to give you two quarter square triangle blocks. Repeat for all ten pairs.
5. Cut the blocks apart on the drawn line (diagram **B**). Open out and press the seams. The blocks should measure 9¼ in/23.5 cm square to the raw edge.
6. Stitch the blocks into four strips of five blocks. Spread one backing strip right side down on a flat surface, then smooth out the wadding. Add the wadding strip and the pieced top strip, right side facing on top. Fasten together with safety pins or baste in a grid (diagram **C**).
7. Hand or machine quilt the layers as desired.

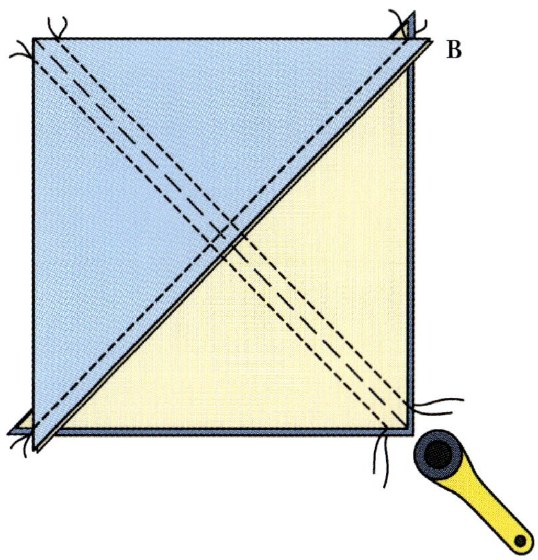
B

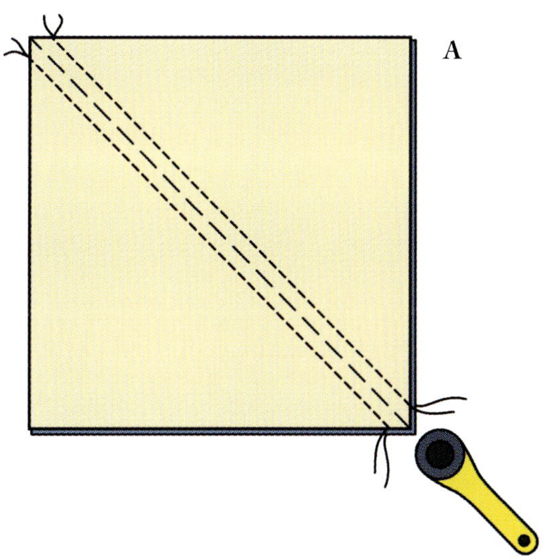
A

C

SASHING STRIPS

1 You will need to piece both sets of sashing strips together so that they are long enough for your strips. Stitch them together with a diagonal seam and press the seam open.

2 Fold the 1⅞ in/4.75 cm wide sashing strip in half with wrong sides facing and press.

3 Align the raw edge of the 1⅛ in/2.75 cm wide sashing strip with the first quilt strip with right sides together. Then place the raw edges of the folded strip on reverse, matching all raw edges. Pin then stitch both sashing strips at the same time to the first quilt strip with a ¼ in/0.75cm seam (diagram **D**).

D

4 Trim the ends of the sashing strips to match the top and bottom edges of the quilt strip.

5 Pin and then stitch the second quilt strip to the raw edge of the 1⅛ in/2.75 cm wide sashing strip with right sides facing (diagram **E**).

E

6 Continue joining your quilt and sashing strips in the same way until the four strips are stitched together.

7 Pin the folded edge of each sashing strip on the back of the quilt top in place to cover the seam allowance and slip stitch in place by hand (diagram **F**). You can also stitch this in place by machine.

F

BINDING

Join the binding strips with diagonal seams to make a continuous length to fit all round the quilt and use to bind the edges with a double-fold binding, mitred at the corners.

NOTE The edges of the two seam allowances should meet in the middle of the sashing strip. If there is a gap between the two edges, increase your seam allowance. If, however, the two edges overlap, decrease your seam allowance.

LOOKED AT ANOTHER WAY

If you are using a Layer Cake pack why not piece both sides in the way described in the method instead of purchasing a coordinating backing to make a pieced reversible quilt.

Stack, Cut & Shuffle

DESIGNED BY MARION PATTERSON

I love using this technique as the quilt grows quickly and it is an ideal way to use up fabrics from your stash. They can either coordinate to give a harmonious look or be totally scrappy – the choice is up to you. Have fun making it.

FINISHED SIZE
40 in x 60 in/101 cm x 150 cm

YOU WILL NEED
All fabrics are 100% cotton

- **Body of the quilt** Eight fat quarters or eight pieces of fabric at least 17 in/ 43.25 cm square
- **Side Setting Triangles and Corner Triangles** Coordinating fabric, 1¼ yds/1.15 mtrs
- **Backing** 48 in x 68 in/ 122 cm x 173 cm
- **Wadding** 48 in x 68 in/ 122 cm x 173 cm
- **Binding** Coordinating fabric, ½ yd/50 cm

CUTTING

1 From your eight chosen fabrics cut eight squares approximately 17 in/43.25 cm square. Stack the fabrics on top of each other on your cutting mat, right side facing up and cut into eight segments. The first cut needs to be from bottom to the top; separate the two halves then each half needs to be cut into four segments. Use diagram A as a guide but it doesn't matter if your shapes look different.

A

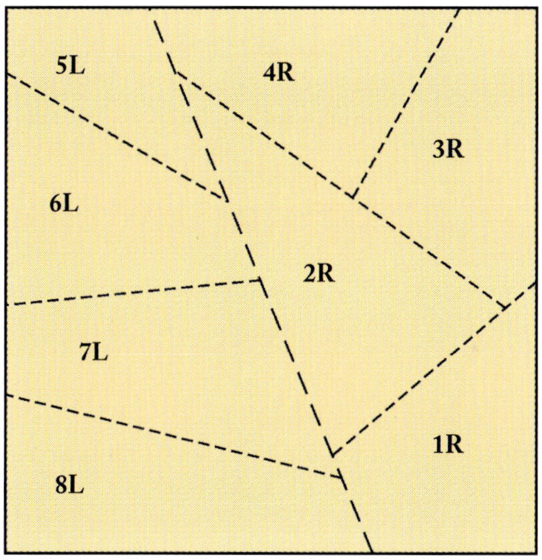

2 Put a piece of paper on each of the segments, mark it with the number 1 to 8 and the letter R or L to show whether it is the right or left segment (diagram **A**). Mix the pieces up in the following order to give the best mix of colours:

1. Move the top piece on stack 1R to the bottom ofthe stack.
2. Move the top two pieceson stack 2R to the bottom of the stack.
3. Move the top three pieces on stack 3R to the bottom of the stack.
4. Move the top four pieces on stack 4R to the bottom of the stack.
5. Move the top five pieces on stack 5L to the bottom of the stack.
6. Move the top six pieces on stack 6L to the bottom of the stack.
7. Move the top seven pieces on stack 7L to the bottom of the stack.
8. **Do not move any of the pieces in stack 8L.**

B

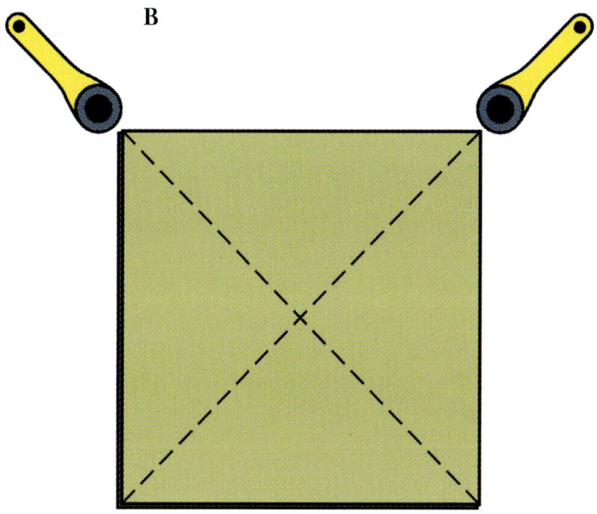

3 From your side setting/corner fabric cut two squares 21 in/53.25 cm then cut each in half diagonally to make eight triangles in all (you will need to use 6 of these). This will ensure the long side of the triangle will not have a bias edge (diagram **B**).

QUILT PLAN

C

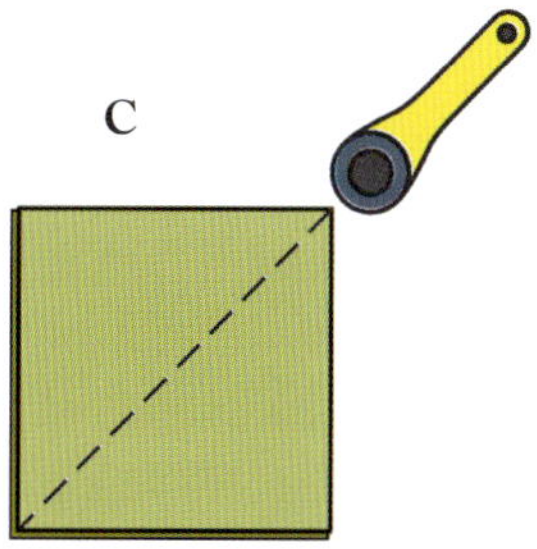

4 Cut two squares 10⅞ in/27.3 cm then cut these in half on the diagonal to make 4 triangles in all (diagram **C**)

5 From the binding fabric, cut six strips 2½ in/6.5 cm wide across the width of the fabric.

E

STITCHING

1 Assemble the blocks in the reverse order of cutting (finger press or iron the seams to one side as you go).

2 Pin then stitch piece 4R to 3R along the cutting line (cut 3), then pin and stitch to pieces 2R and 1R (cuts 2 and 1). This is the right side of the block completed.

3 Now pin and stitch piece 8L to 7L along the cutting line (cut 6), then pin and stitch to pieces 6L and 5L (cuts 5 and 4). This completes your left side of the block.

4 If you have an uneven edge along the left and right joining side of the block, trim this to give you a straight edge to enable you to stitch the left and right sides of the block together.

D

5 Piece the segments for all eight blocks in this way. Once all the blocks have been stitched and pressed, trim the block down to 14½ in/37 cm square (diagram **D**).

6 Following the quilt plan on page 124 or diagram **E** above, attach the side setting triangles to the blocks. Stitch the diagonal rows together and attach the corner setting triangles.

FINISHING

1 Mark your quilting design on the quilt. Your quilt is now ready for layering.

2 Spread the backing right side down on a flat surface, then working from the centre outwards, smooth out the wadding and the patchwork top, right side up, on top. Fasten together with safety pins or baste in a grid.

3 Hand or machine quilt the layers.

BINDING

Stitch all the binding strips into one length and use to bind the quilt with a double-fold binding, mitred at the corners.

LOOKED AT ANOTHER WAY

If you wanted to make the quilt larger, you could add one or more borders to the quilt top until you have the desired size. Alternatively, you could add more blocks and borders. If you decide to make the blocks themselves larger, however, you will need to alter the size of the side setting triangles and the corner triangles.

Useful addresses

Visit your local quilt or craft store, or an online supplier, for a variety of fabric, threads and tools.

UK

Marion's Patchworks
www.marionspatchworks.co.uk
Tel: 01792 416833
(patchwork, quilting and needlecraft suppliers)

Busy Bees
www.busybeespatchwork.co.uk
Tel: 01633 810801
(patchwork, quilting and needlecraft suppliers)

Abigail Crafts
www.abigailcrafts.co.uk
Tel: 01453 823691
(patchwork and embroidery suppliers)

Patchwork Direct
www.patchworkdirect.com
Tel: 01629 734100
(patchwork and quilting suppliers)

Quilt Room
www.quiltroom.com
Tel: 01306 877307
(patchwork and quilting suppliers)

The Cloth House
www.clothhouse.com
Tel: 020 7437 5155
(fabric suppliers)

US

Great suppliers of quilt-making materials in the United States are too numerous to list here, so please consult your favorite retailer or online vendor!

Index

The Contributors

Marion Patterson runs an online quilting shop and also organises a quilting workshop programme.

Sally Ablett designs for a quilt fabric manufacturer and gives workshops around the UK.

Sue Warren co-owns a quilting shop in Newport, Wales, as well as organises workshop programmes.